CAMBERWELL
COUNCIL
ON ALCOHOLISM

Women &

Alcohol

TAVISTOCK PUBLICATIONS
LONDON AND NEW YORK

First published in 1980 by
Tavistock Publications Ltd
11 New Fetter Lane, London EC4P 4EE
Published in the USA by
Tavistock Publications
in association with Methuen, Inc.
733 Third Avenue, New York, NY 10017

Typeset by Red Lion Setters, London
Printed in Great Britain by
Richard Clay (The Chaucer Press) Ltd,
Bungay, Suffolk

British Library Cataloguing in Publication Data

Camberwell Council on Alcoholism
  Women and alcohol.
  1. Alcohol and women
  I. Title
  362.2'92   HV5137   80-40370

  ISBN 0-422-76950-9
  ISBN 0-422-76960-6 Pbk

Women &
Alcohol

Contents

To Astor Balfour Sclare
who died during the preparation of
the manuscript

Acknowledgements

The authors would like to thank the following people and organizations for their particular support and assistance:

Staff and patients at Scalebor Park Alcoholism Treatment Unit;
National Cyrenians;
Members of the Camberwell Council on Alcoholism Executive Committee and Officers;
All who have been members of the C.C.A. Women and Alcohol Action Group and of the sub-group on problems of detection;
Our friends and colleagues who have given us so much of their time and interest as well as valuable information;
Adrienne Boyle, Diane Hallett, Pat Davis, Di Harding, and Jean Crutch who prepared the final manuscripts.

Introduction

'My experience as an alcoholic, as a counsellor of women alcoholics, and as a sociologist has led me to define what I found to be different; women have low or no self esteem; women have extreme feelings of guilt; women experience much depression; women, more often than not must combat their alcoholism alone, nine out of ten husbands leaving them. There is no male equivalent to the drinking housewife. Women suffer not only from alcoholism but role identification. Women lack a clear image of their role as women, our culture having created much of the confusion. Women alcoholics feel that they have failed as wives, as mothers, as women. They feel guilty because society makes them feel so. All women live in a sexist society. Alcoholic women also carry the stigma of being an unladylike drunk.'

> Jean Kirkpatrick, Phd., President, Women for Sobriety Inc., from a letter to Senator William Hathaway, Sub-Committee on Alcoholism and Narcotics.

'Let's face it – there really is nothing manly or heroic or glamorous about those who drink too much. In men it is crude and embarrassing: in women it is plain sickening.'

> Mr David Ennals, Secretary of State for Social Services at the opening of the Health Education Council's North East Campaign on Alcohol Education.

This book attempts to draw together current ideas and information about alcohol use and drinking problems amongst women. Until fairly recently information on women's drinking problems was scattered throughout the literature on alcoholism; although work had been done with women, it was often as part of a larger study primarily concerned with men, and the question of differences between men and women alcoholics was largely ignored. The last ten years, however, have seen a rapid increase in interest in alcoholism amongst women from the perspective of both research and treatment. Literature reviews and the growing body of research on women alcoholics have indicated clearly that the situation for the sexes is qualitatively different with regard to alcohol use and alcohol-related problems, and that this has important implications for the way in which the 'helping professions' respond to men and women with drinking problems and the kind of treatment services which are offered to them.

It is not possible, nor desirable, to put together the diverse information that exists without attempting to provide a perspective by which to understand what is known and what is not. Our perspective broadly concerns the importance of the gender of the alcoholic, for we would argue that female alcoholism can only be effectively understood in the context of the situation of women in our society. For example, the sexual stereotypes that inform people's expectations as to acceptable or unacceptable behaviour crucially influence how women and men perceive the use of alcohol and the way they express the problems they may have with alcohol abuse. Where possible, we have drawn from both academic literature and practical experience and we have given practical suggestions about what should improve, for example, the early detection of women with drinking problems and the consequent counselling of them.

This book is intended to be useful to anyone with a professional or personal interest in drinking and drinking problems amongst women, and in the role of women in our society. Each chapter deals with an aspect of alcoholism in women and is as complete as possible on its own. The book is organized so that it can be read as a whole and it has been designed to minimize overlap across chapters and to present ideas within a common perspective.

The book is presented under the auspices of the Camberwell Council on Alcoholism because it was responsible for the thinking behind the book, calling the group of authors together and, most importantly, supported them both as individuals and as a collective.

The Camberwell Council on Alcoholism (C.C.A.)

The C.C.A. was set up in the early 1960s and was the first of its kind in Great Britain. It is based in South London, England, and is concerned to obtain the range of services necessary to help people with drinking problems or those affected by the drinking of others, in the two inner London Boroughs of Southwark and Lambeth; this work entails campaigning for services and finding ways of educating lay and professional people about the nature and consequences of alcohol abuse.

The C.C.A. has not always been so locally minded for it has been key in the setting up of two national non-statutory agencies (one to provide education for those working with problem drinkers, the other to co-ordinate day centres and residential facilities) and a local counselling service based on a model of provision designed to ensure that the services are an integral part of the local community.

The Council's concern with female alcoholism arose, in the early 1970s, out of discussions with local agencies about recent changes in the number of women being referred to them. Members of the Council were worried that so little was understood about how best to meet the needs of these women. As a result, a series of seminars for local lay and professional people were arranged and were so successful that an action group was set up with a brief to arrange further events of this nature. This group met, almost every week, for four years, from 1974 to 1978. Throughout this time, members (who amounted, over a time, to thirty people) gave lectures at both national and international events, organized training courses, set up a re-print library, wrote pamphlets and articles on a range of issues, and ultimately were responsible, with others, for setting up Drugs, Alcohol and Women Nationally (D.A.W.N.), whose purpose is to co-ordinate and channel efforts to obtain for women who are alcohol and drug-abusers services to assist them and which are their right.

Four of the authors were members of the C.C.A. action group, the rest have at some time, been associated with it because of their specialist knowledge and interest.

1

STAN SHAW

Co-director
Detoxification Evaluation Project
Maudsley Hospital, London

The causes of increasing drinking problems amongst women: a general etiological theory

Virtually every contemporary report on the prevalence of drinking problems mentions that drinking problems are increasing, and increasing most among women. This chapter will be no exception, but unlike other reports, this present chapter will go on to attempt a general theoretical explanation as to why this should be so.

Evidence of increasing prevalence amongst women

Four sets of statistics have typically been taken as indicators of trends in the prevalence of drinking problems: (i) drunkenness offence rates, (ii) numbers receiving treatment for drinking problems, (iii) liver cirrhosis mortality, and (iv) alcoholic mortality. Over recent years, the rate of increase of these indicators has been greater amongst women than amongst men.

2 Women & Alcohol

(i) DRUNKENNESS OFFENCES

(a) drunkenness

Although male drunken offenders heavily outnumber female offenders, female drunkenness has been increasing at a greater rate than male drunkenness. For example, between 1975 and 1976 male drunkenness rose 3 per cent, but the number of offences amongst women rose 14 per cent. *Table 1* traces this development over a ten-year period.

Table 1 *Findings of guilt for drunkenness offences in England and Wales 1967-1976*

	number		female offences as % of all offences
year	males	females	
1967	71,167	4,377	5·8
1968	74,226	4,844	6·1
1969	75,472	5,030	6·3
1970	77,072	5,302	6·4
1971	81,006	5,729	6·6
1972	84,168	6,030	6·7
1973	92,974	6,300	6·3
1974	92,294	6,909	6·7
1975	96,880	7,572	7·2
1976	100,056	8,642	8·0

Sources: Chief Constables' Reports 1977 Pt. 1, Drink Offences (Christian Economic and Social Research Foundation 25th *Annual Report*); *Offences of Drunkenness* (1976) HMSO Cmnd. 6952 (1977).

(b) drinking and driving

Women are even more outnumbered in the drinking and driving statistics. They accounted for only 1 per cent of offenders in 1968, the first year of the breathalyser, but have climbed steadily each year up to 3 per cent of offences by 1977, whilst male offences have recently fallen away.

Table 2   *Convictions for drinking and driving in England and Wales, 1968-77*

| year | number | | female offences as % of all offences |
	males	females	
1968	18,183	201	1·1
1969	23,417	304	1·3
1970	25,930	343	1·3
1971	38,207	567	1·5
1972	46,382	716	1·5
1973	54,077	976	1·8
1974	55,033	1,120	2·0
1975	56,757	1,388	2·4
1976	48,651	1,348	2·7
1977	43,966	1,403	3·1

*1968 was the first full year in which the breathalyser was operative under the provisions of the *Road Safety Act* which came into force on 9 October, 1967.
Sources: Home Office; Department of the Environment: extrapolated from The Brewers' Society (1978).

(ii)   TREATMENT FOR DRINKING PROBLEMS

(a)   alcoholism admissions

The number of males diagnosed as alcoholics doubled in the decade from 1964 to 1975, but the number of females trebled. Thus whilst male alcoholics in mental illness hospitals in England and Wales outnumbered women by four to one in 1964, the ratio by 1975 had become nearer 2·5 men to every woman.

(b)   membership of Alcoholics Anonymous (AA)

Because of its principle of anonymity, and lack of formal structure, AA publishes no official annual membership figures. Nevertheless, three surveys have been conducted over the years. In 1964, a survey of London AA Groups (Edwards *et al*, 1967)

Table 3   *Admissions to mental illness hospitals and units in England with a diagnosis of alcoholism or alcoholic psychosis 1964, and 1970-75*

| year | admissions | | ratio |
	male	female	male : female
1964	4,030	1,043	3·9:1
1970	5,232	1,594	3·3:1
1971	6,111	1,721	3·6:1
1972	6,758	2,033	3·3:1
1973	7,626	2,367	3·2:1
1974	8,049	2,793	2·9:1
1975	8,144	3,028	2·7:1

Source: Department of Health and Social Security (DHSS) DHSS Mental Health Inquiry. Reproduced in C. Wilson (1976).

found a ratio of four men to every women member. By 1972 a small unpublished survey by the General Service Board of AA itself (Alcoholics Anonymous 1972) reported that there were three men to every woman. In late 1976 a national survey of AA membership (Robinson, 1979) found a ratio of only two men to every woman in the fellowship. Furthermore, amongst members who had been in AA for less than four years, there were as many women as there were men (Robinson 1979). Now there are even some exclusively female AA groups. The changing ratio of membership of AA has thus mirrored almost exactly the changing ratio in admissions to psychiatric hospitals for alcoholism treatment.

A survey of over 13,000 AA members in North America in 1975 showed that women made up 28 per cent of AA members in the USA and Canada, compared with 26 per cent in 1971 and 22 per cent in 1968 (*Alliance News*, 1975). Again the increasing incidence amongst women was demonstrated in that one third of all new members in North America between 1972 and 1975 were female.

(c)   presentation to alcohol counselling services

Counselling services for people with drinking problems have

primarily been provided in the UK by local Councils on Alcoholism. Because these services have been sporadic, and have been established at different times, trends cannot be discerned with precision. Nevertheless, at the beginning of 1970, the ratio of men to women presenting at such services in Merseyside, Manchester, and Glasgow was about six to one, but by 1975 this had become three to one (Wilson, 1976). One local Council on Alcoholism reported that half its clients were women (Somerset Council on Alcoholism, 1975). Since 1975, the general incidence of women presenting to counselling services has continued to rise. One service reported that its ratio of two men to every woman in 1976 and 1977, had become two women for every three men by 1978 (Accept, 1977). The national picture by 1977 was that new clients to local Councils on Alcoholism affiliated to the National Council on Alcoholism, comprised 1,666 males and 620 females, a ratio of 2·7:1.

(iii) LIVER CIRRHOSIS MORTALITY

For reasons, which will briefly be explained later in this chapter, and more fully in the next, the rates of females suffering liver damage have always been closer to that of males than rates of alcoholism treatment. Thus, the ratio of increase amongst females dying from cirrhosis is not as striking as amongst the other figures.

Table 4 *Deaths in England and Wales from cirrhosis of the liver, and death rate per million*

| year | males | | females | | M:F ratio |
	number	rate per million	number	rate per million	
1970	741	31·36	651	25·98	1·1:1
1971	806	33·96	764	30·42	1·1:1
1972	858	35·99	804	31·91	1·1:1
1973	943	39·43	861	34·09	1·1:1
1975	920	38·44	915	36·27	1·0:1

Source: Office of Population Censuses and Surveys. Reproduced in *Annual Abstract of Statistics* (1976), HMSO.

(IV) DEATHS CERTIFIED AS DUE TO ALCOHOLISM
AND ALCOHOLIC PSYCHOSIS

It has long been recognised that doctors and coroners are loath
to certify death as being due to alcoholism or alcoholic psychosis, and so the figures below are almost certainly underestimates.
Yet these statistics mirror cirrhosis mortality in that the number
of females is almost the same as the number of males.

Table 5   *Deaths certified as due to alcoholism and alcoholic psychosis
in England and Wales, 1973-1975*

year	male	female	M:F ratio
1973	103	49	2·1:1
1974	129	61	2·1:1
1975	118	81	1·5:1

Source: Office of Population Censuses and Surveys. Reproduced in *Annual
Abstract of Statistics* (1976), HMSO.

The general picture from all these figures over the last decade,
then, is of a general rising prevalence of various indicators of
drinking problems, with a rate of increase amongst females
being greater than that amongst males, especially among the
more sensitive indicators of drunkenness offences and numbers
in treatment. Furthermore, although the figures presented
pertain largely to Britain, the same phenomenon has been noted
in Europe and in North America (Curlee, 1967; Whitehead and
Ferrence, 1976).

Interpreting the increasing prevalence rates

Although the trend towards more alcohol-related problems
amongst women, as indicated by all the above statistics, seems
plain enough, nevertheless these statistics should be treated with
a degree of caution. For it might be argued that the prevalence of
alcohol problems amongst women have not increased at all, but
rather the changing social climate and the increasing publicity
and education about drinking problems have made it easier for
women to admit to having drinking problems, and to present

themselves for help and treatment. Furthermore it may be that other labelling agencies such as the police and doctors have become more aware of drinking problems amongst women, and are now more ready to recognize and to label them as drunks or alcoholics. The expanding availability of counselling and psychiatric alcoholism services since the early 1960s might also have encouraged more help-seeking by women and more referrals of women.

However, there are very sound reasons for believing that even if these factors may partly account for some of the rises, nevertheless there has been a *real* increase in drinking problems amongst women. For although each rate of increase might in itself be of dubious validity, when each rate presents the same basic picture, then a degree of concurrent validity can be assumed. Indeed the close similarity in the changing sex ratio of presentations to psychiatric alcoholic services, Alcoholics Anonymous, and counselling services – three very different types of service with different means of entry – suggests that this change in ratio is a general trend and not specific to the availability of some particular type of service or an artifact of the idiosyncratic data collection.

As for drunkenness figures, it is more probable that they underestimate the true incidence of female public drunkenness. In the first place the police are more likely to choose to caution women rather than men as an alternative to arrest. In 1976, female offences were one tenth those of men, but the number of women cautioned for drunkenness with no proceedings following was only a quarter that of men (HMSO, 1977: 406 males were cautioned, compared to 125 females). Second, once arrested, women are more likely than men to be found not guilty. In 1976, 2·7 per cent of proceedings against males for drunkenness offences returned not guilty verdicts, compared to 3·3 per cent of females.

The etiology of drinking problems

More important than these arguments about the validity of statistics is the fact that the increased prevalence of alcohol-related problems amongst women can be interpreted as a true increase because a whole range of factors known to be associated with women's drinking and drinking problems have changed in a way likely to increase women's alcohol consumption and their experience of drinking problems. Indeed this will be the core argument of this chapter.

Until recently, the study of alcoholism and drinking problems has lacked a general etiological theory, that is, an overall framework by which to assess the relative importance of the many different possible causes of drinking problems. Indeed, during the years in which the disease concept of alcoholism held sway, it was simply assumed that the causes of drinking problems were internal to the drinker and lay in some personality predisposition or biochemical freak, which made some people allergic to alcohol and hence unable to control their drinking. Since this allergy was presumed incurable, the only recourse for alcoholics was to become totally abstinent. The general acceptance of this theory meant that etiological study of the causes of drinking problems was thought unimportant in either understanding or treating drinking problems.

On the other hand, another school of thought (De Lint and Schmidt, 1971) arose which suggested that the overall prevalence in drinking problems was simply determined by the overall level of alcohol consumption, since those societies with the highest consumption also reported the highest number of alcoholics and liver cirrhosis deaths.

In recent years, both these perspectives have been challenged. The disease concept of alcoholism has been criticized as a mystified and inflexible view of the problem, and exhaustive research has failed to find any biochemical allergy or single personality disposition which this theory supposed caused alcoholism. (Shaw *et al.*, 1978). At the same time the statistical and mathematical theorems that implicated increasing consumption as the major causal factor in increasing drink problems have become equally questioned (Miller and Agnew, 1974; Duffy, 1977). In effect, both of these theories contain important messages but by themselves they are incomplete explanations. For all the evidence collected over recent years has demonstrated that the causes of drinking problems are multifactorial, involving social, economic, psychological, and physiological factors. This wide range of factors not only determine why, what, and when people drink, but they also determine how far people are protected against, or vulnerable to, problems from their drinking pattern. Thus a recent review of trends (Cartwright and Shaw, 1978) in this multi factorial school of thought about drinking problems has conceptualized current thinking about the causes of drinking problems in the following diagrammatic way:

Figure 1   The etiology of drinking problems

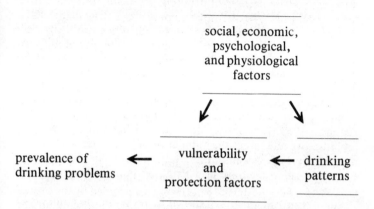

Source: Reproduced from Cartwright and Shaw (1978).

Changes in women's drinking patterns

We should begin by considering the right hand side of the equation, – how women's drinking patterns have changed – since at other times and in other societies, increases in the rates of official statistics, such as drunkenness arrests and alcoholism admissions, have been found invariably to occur in times of increasing general consumption of alcohol. The number of problems from drinking reported by individual people have also been shown to be related to their individual consumption level. The more people drink, the greater risk they begin to run of experiencing various types of alcohol-related problems (Shaw *et al.*, 1978). For instance, when surveys are conducted to find problem drinkers in the community, they usually pick up less women problem drinkers than men. A survey in a South London suburb identified twenty-five out of 408 men as problem drinkers compared with only four out of 520 women. But it was also found that the average consumption of women was much lower than that of men, and the researchers concluded that, 'The strongest hypothesis to explain differences in the male and female problem rates seems on present evidence to be that this difference is to be understood as very closely related to underlying sex differences in normal drinking patterns'. For when men and women who drank around the same amount were compared, there was found to be no significant difference in the number of problems they reported. Indeed, we shall see later, women are actually at greater risk than men from the same amount of alcohol consumption. So in 1965 it appeared that 'we have it seems to ask not why women experience less trouble but why women drink less' (Edwards, Hensman, and Peto, 1972: 124).

However, since we have now seen that problems amongst women are rising, the question becomes different to that one posed in 1965. If problems have been rising amongst women, and if, as we have seen, the number of problems is related to the average level of consumption, we should now be asking if it is the case that women are now drinking more on average than previously, and if so why?

Surveys in America have shown increases in the numbers of women drinkers. In 1946, 75 per cent of US men drank on some occasions compared with 56 per cent of women (Riley and Marden, 1947). In 1969, the figures had risen to 77 per cent of men drinking compared with 60 per cent of women – each percentage point representing approximately one million people (Cahalan, Cisin, and Crossley, 1969). Furthermore, recent survey data has shown a tendency for more American women to move from the light drinking category into the category of moderate consumption (Room, 1972).

In Britain, women's drinking patterns have undergone a more dramatic change, particularly in the 1970s. Indeed, the drinks sales executive of International Publishing Corporation (IPC) Womens Magazines has concluded that 'the growth among women drinkers is the most significant factor affecting the drink market as a whole' (Ratcliffe, 1979: 6).

In brief, the overall trends in the UK were that alcohol consumption rose markedly from 1960 to 1969, accelerated massively from 1969 to 1974, and then fell slightly up to 1976 and regained slightly from 1976 to 1979. There were noticeable differences in different areas of the market. The table below shows the relative percentage increase over the main watershed years in the consumption of beer, spirits, and wine.

Table 6   *Percentage increase in UK alcohol consumption 1960-79 by type of drink*

type of drink	1960-69 % increase	1969-74 % increase	1974-79 % increase
beer	21·3	20·4	4·6
wine	94·5	83·4	14·3
spirits	25·0	86·8	27·7

Source: HM Customs and Excise. Extrapolated from The Brewers' Society (1978).

Women are relatively unimportant in beer consumption, which has risen only marginally over the last two decades. Spirits consumption increased at about the same slow rate in the 1960s, but increased markedly more in the first half of the 1970s. Furthermore, it increased most in those sections of the spirits market where women increased their consumption of white rum, gin, and vodka. But the real growth market has been in wine, where consumption virtually doubled from 1960 to 1969, and then nearly doubled again in a mere five years up to 1974, and this is precisely the sector of the drinks market where women have become the dominant purchasers and consumers.

This market comprises fortified wine (e.g. sherry and port), vermouths (e.g. Cinzano, Martini), and table wines. An IPC survey in 1976 (*Alliance News*, Jan/Feb, 1977) showed that more women bought sherry than men – 54 per cent to 46 per cent – and a subsequent survey in 1978 showed that 'women are involved in a staggering 86 per cent of decisions to buy sherry for the home' (Ratcliffe 1979: 7). The same survey showed that between 1969/70 and 1976/77, the vermouth market grew 118 per cent. In the same period, the number of women vermouth drinkers rose by 140 per cent, so that by the time of the survey,

63 per cent of all the products in this rapidly expanding sector was being consumed by women.

Even more significant has been the increased consumption of table wine by women. The IPC 1976 survey noted that 'the ladies have become the major factor in the increasing prosperity of the wine trade' (*Alliance News*, 1977: 11). Another survey in 1976, conducted for the Co-operative Wholesale Society showed that although men actually made 56 per cent (*Alliance News*, 1976) of the purchases of table wine, women consumers outnumbered men by 9½m to 8½m. The 1978 IPC study showed that from 1969/70 to 1976/77, table wine sales rose 45 per cent and the number of women consumers rose by 55 per cent and confirmed that more table wine was being consumed by women than by men (Ratcliffe, 1979).

These developments concur with the evidence from epidemiological studies that an increase in consumption in any group is not usually the outcome of complete alterations in drinking habits, but rather a cumulative effect of adding new elements, such as different types of drink and different drinking situations to an already existing pattern (Sulkunen, 1976; Makela, 1975). In this sense, women's drinking habits in the UK have not so much changed as had new elements superimposed upon them.

The increasing availability of alcohol to women

Epidemiological studies of the prevalence of drinking problems have always concurred that an increase in per capita consumption in a social group has invariably been related to the increased availability of alcohol, particularly in economic terms, to that group (De Lint and Schmidt, 1971). Increased economic availability, which makes increased consumption more likely, has two dimensions: (i) reduced real price of alcohol and (ii) wider distribution outlets.

(i) REDUCED REAL PRICE OF ALCOHOL

Some studies have shown that the consumption of alcohol is almost exactly related to its price as a proportion of real disposable income, i.e. the amount which people have got to spend. Whenever the real price of alcohol falls as a proportion of disposable income, then alcohol consumption rises (De Lint and Schmidt, 1971).

In the case of women in the UK over recent years, both factors have come into operation. For the real price of alcohol has declined at the same time as women's disposable income has been increasing.

It has been calculated that between 1967 and 1977, for a blue-collar man aged twenty-one or over on average earnings and working full-time in a manufacturing industry, after tax had been deducted at the standard rate, the real price of beer fell 4 per cent, the real price of wines fell 14 per cent, and the real price of spirits fell 21 per cent (Accept, 1977). So those sections of the market that fell most in real price, namely wines and spirits, were the same markets in which women's purchasing and consumption became most noticeable. The drinks most attractive to women fell most in real price. Furthermore, as the real price of wines and spirits was falling, women's income was increasing. The table below shows that in 1972, the average weekly earnings of women were 56 per cent those of men. However, between 1972 and 1977, the average weekly earnings of men rose 104 per cent but women's rose 147 per cent, with the result that by 1977 women's average weekly earnings were 65 per cent those of men.

The median (i.e. the typical) average wage of women actually trebled between 1972 and 1977.

Table 7   *Average weekly earnings of full-time workers in all industries, 1972-77*

year	men £	women £
1972	36·0	20·1
1973	40·9	22·6
1974	46·5	26·3
1975	59·2	36·6
1976	70·0	45·3
1977	76·8	50·0

Source: Department of Employment. Condensed from *Annual Abstract of Statistics* (1978), HMSO.

The influence of rising income may be especially important in the case of women, since American surveys have shown that the percentage of men who drink is higher amongst lower income than among higher income groups, but the opposite is true of women. The higher the income bracket, the less women abstain from drinking (Lawrence and Maxwell, 1962; Knupfer and Room, 1964). It may also be that women have achieved a greater flexibility of choice over their disposable income over recent years, with less married couples adopting a system of the man giving the wife a fixed amount simply to cover housekeeping.

Not only have women's average weekly earnings been increasing faster than men's, but the disposable income of women as a group has increased still further because more of them have been coming into employment. The number of women entering employment has been increasing whilst the male working population has actually been decreasing. By mid-1972, there were for the first time over nine million women working, and by mid-June 1977, this had risen to over ten million. The numbers of women relative to men is displayed in *Table 8* below.

Table 8   *Total UK working population in thousands in selected years 1968-1977*

year	males	females	M:F ratio
	(in thousands)		
1968	16,563	8,814	1·9:1
1971	16,219	8,904	1·8:1
1974	16,001	9,601	1·7:1
1977	16,261	10,066	1·6:1

Source: Department of Employment. Condensed from *Annual Abstract of Statistics* (1978) HMSO.

The combined effect of both the working population of women and their average weekly earnings increasing at a faster rate than those of men has meant a considerably faster increase in the real disposable income of women as a whole than men.

The Department of Employment (Information Division of the Treasury 1974: 2) have pointed out

> 'the causes of these developments are complex and not all can be quantified. With smaller families and less time between children, the period of time while a woman has children under school age is considerably reduced, and her total absence from the work force through bringing up her family is much shorter than in previous generations. It is also now more socially acceptable for a woman with dependent children to be in employment.'

Moreover 'mass production and advances in technology have combined to . . . reduce the amount of time necessary to carry out basic domestic chores. The service industries also have developed to cater increasingly for the needs of the working woman.'

The fact of being employed appears to put women at greater risk of contracting drinking problems. A study of alcoholism in an urban residential area found that 48 per cent of all women worked, but 67 per cent of women with drinking problems worked (Bailey, Haberman, and Alksne, 1965). Some women work in fields with a high risk of contracting drinking problems, such as journalism and other media positions, marketing, representative work, advertising, managerial and personnel positions with considerable responsibility, and have in these instances become exposed to the same stresses and pressures that have applied to men in these situations. Indeed, the pressures may even be greater on women when they are carrying out a dual role of breadwinner and housewife and mother.

Some occupations carry a risk of increasing consumption of alcohol simply because drink is freely or cheaply available or readily to hand. The most obvious example is the increasing number of women working in public houses, where most of them work as barmaids. *Table 9* below demonstrates that the female percentage of the working population in pubs and clubs was 59·5 per cent in 1963 but had risen to 68 per cent by 1978, by which time there were 129,000 more women working in pubs and clubs than men. In 1978, there were over twice as many women working in pubs as men.

Table 9   *Employees in public houses and clubs in selected years, 1963-1978*

year	public houses			clubs		
	men	women	M:F	men	women	M:F
	(thousands)		*ratio*	*(thousands)*		*ratio*
1963	58	92	1:1·6	33	42	1:1·3
1966	62	96	1:1·6	35	44	1:1·3
1969	64	92	1:1·4	36	42	1:1·2
1972	67	121	1:1·8	35	52	1:1·6
1975	78	152	1:2·0	39	60	1:1·5
1978	76	177	1:2·3	40	68	1:1·7

Source: Department of Employment. Extrapolated from The Brewers' Society (1978).

(ii) WIDER DISTRIBUTION OUTLETS

The second form of increased economic availability lies in changes in the retail distribution of alcoholic drink which make the purchase of alcohol easier and more convenient. The most important developments making alcohol more accessible to women derived from the 1961 *Licencing Act* which allowed off-licences to open during normal shopping hours, followed by the abolition of retail price maintenance on alcoholic drinks in 1966/67, which encouraged grocery store chains and super-markets to open drinks departments on their existing premises. By 1977 half of Britain's supermarkets had licences to sell alcohol. The result was that suddenly women had available to them numerous places for purchasing alcohol in the non-stigmatic context of their ordinary shopping (*Annual Abstract of Statistics*, 1978). It has become much easier, more imper-sonal, and more 'respectable' for women to obtain alcohol at a supermarket than it had been in pubs and even in off-licences.

A survey in 1975 by Gordon Simmons Research (Otto, 1977) found that licenced stores accounted for 42 per cent of all take-home alcohol sales, and off-licences for 40 per cent and that as many women as men were purchasing drinks in licenced stores. Recent figures have indicated that women have now become more important than men for the bulk of purchases from licenced stores. IPC Woman's Market magazine stated in 1976 that 'with grocery outlets accounting for almost half the current £860m. drinks trade, it is clear women have become the big spenders in the alcoholic drinks market' (Otto, 1977: 25).

Social factors in the increasing availability of alcohol to women

Besides the economic factors making alcohol relatively cheaper and more accessible to women, there are also other more subtle factors which have made alcohol more available to women.

First, women have become able to drink more often and to drink more when they do, because it has become a more socially acceptable, and indeed fashionable and approved, behaviour for women. The social milieu has been moving towards a more permissive drinking culture for women, and the decrease in social constraints upon women's drinking must be seen in a symbiotic relationship with the changing economic factors. The most obvious example of this is the increasing likelihood of women drinking in pubs, clubs, and bars. At one time women in public houses used to be frowned upon, unless accompanied by men, and in general such places were designed for, and likely to be populated by, men. A survey by IPC Marketing Services showed that by 1975, 55 per cent of women used pubs (compared to 76 per cent of men) (Otto, 1977). The *Financial Times* reported in 1976 that brewers had spent heavily on public houses to make them more attractive to women. Women going out in pairs and groups to pubs and other drinking situations has become a much more regular feature. Although there is some disapproval of women alone in a pub, in most places women are certainly unquestioningly accepted in single sex or mixed company groups.

Indeed, they would appear especially acceptable to landlords, since it has recently been reported that pubs with a higher than average proportion of women have higher than average sales. In pubs where over 40 per cent of customers are female, turnover is 43 per cent above average (National Council on Alcoholism, 1979). Since social drinking by women is increasingly acceptable, this applies to the home as well, where drinking by women in mixed company and all-women groups is considered perfectly respectable now in most sectors of society.

Advertising aimed at women

A similar changing social and economic climate can be found in drinks advertising. There may be some doubt as to whether advertising or redecorating pubs can create social trends, but there is little doubt that it reflects and reinforces existing trends. Trends in advertising have certainly emphasized the increasing importance of women as a consumer group, increased the fashionability of women drinking, and promoted the ideas of women drinking, going into pubs and other drinking situations, and trying out more varied types of drink. In 1972, the total annual bill for the advertising of alcoholic drinks was estimated at between £25m. to £30m. (Home Office, 1972). An increasing proportion of this very large amount of pro-drink propaganda has been directed at women, reinforcing the existing trends toward their increased consumption. *Family Circle*, the grocery trade's own consumer paper, recently remarked that 'drinks companies are at last becoming aware of the growth of supermarket off-licences and the importance of women in the buying decision' (Ratcliffe, 1979: 6).

Family Circle and its stablemate *Living* have, in common with other women's magazines, 'seen an increase in the drinks based advertising during the past couple of years' (Ratcliffe 1979: 6). *Homes and Gardens* (December 1978) carried advertisements for sixteen different brands of alcoholic drink. As might be expected, the drinks advertized in women's magazines tend to be table wines, sherries, aperitifs, liqueurs, and vermouths. Benedictine's advertising agency, for example, which aims its advertising at women, says that 'women are more important than men in the sales of liqueurs' (National Council of Women 1976: 19). Bols, one of the world's largest producers of liqueurs, have reorientated their advertising from TV to women's magazines and even Guinness, who reckon that at least 30 per cent of their customers are women, were spending £150,000 in 1976 on advertising in women's magazines (National Council of Women, 1976). It is not surprising then, that *Supermarketing* should have noted in 1979 that 'it seems inevitable that drinks companies will move more and more into women's magazines' (Ratcliffe 1979: 7). Moreover, other types of advertising media such as newspapers, posters, TV, and radio have also become more geared to catching the woman customer. The expanding vermouth market, highly significant in the changes in women's drinking habits, has featured in consistently lavish TV campaigns. Indeed, drink advertisements on TV and in the cinema have been the subject of considerable criticism because of their portrayal of women who drink as worldly-wise, fashionable, beautiful, sexually attractive, and successful. They were dull and naive until they discovered Smirnoff. These criticisms resulted in a new code of practice from the Advertising Standards Authority in February 1975 by which 'situation' advertizing has been restricted. Nevertheless, it still remains true that many millions of pounds annually are spent attempting to influence women to drink more.

Increasing drinking problems as the ransom of emancipation

Although some writers have considered economic and availability factors to be the dominant issue in determining the overall patterns of prevalence, recent epidemiological thinking as represented by our earlier diagram, has come to recognize that the economic factors discussed so far, although undoubtedly crucial, must be seen within the context of other etiological factors that affect both drinking patterns and drinking problems. It would be a very one-sided argument that attributed the rise in the number of women problem drinkers solely to the increased availability of alcohol to women. We have already seen that this is but a part of wide-sweeping socio-economic changes in which women have become more important consumers with greater financial flexibility and economic independence – changes that have in turn triggered off reinforcing factors such as the increasing advertizing aimed at women.

We must go on to consider these socio-economic changes within the still broader context of the considerable growth of women's social and psychological freedom over recent years. Financial emancipation is part and parcel of social emancipation, and just as economic emancipation has led to increased indulgence in alcohol, so might have greater general social freedom for women. For with greater freedom of choice and opportunity comes more responsibility and more risk. Indeed, one interpretation has been that 'alcoholism represents the ransom woman pays for her emancipation' (Massot, Hamel, and Deliry, 1956: 265).

Broad prevalence factors such as the price of alcohol, and its distribution determine how drinking patterns change overall, but they do not explain specifically why one woman begins to drink a great deal and develops problems, and another does not, when the economic factors applying to them both are identical. So we must go on to consider the other factors in the apex of our etiological diagram which also help to determine drinking patterns, namely social, psychological, and physiological factors. We must consider whether any factors in these areas have changed in ways which might have caused increased consumption and problems amongst women.

In studies of women problem drinkers, and the causes of their problems, four main groups of psychosocial factors have been implicated recurrently. These are that women's drinking problems often seem to be triggered by (i) general stress, (ii) specific life events, (iii) difficulties over role ambiguity, and (iv) difficulties over sociosexual self image. We shall examine each of these in turn and discuss whether there is any evidence to suggest that these range of factors may have come to bear more strongly upon women over recent years, and thus been instrumental in raising the prevalence of drinking problems amongst women.

(i)   GENERAL STRESS

Sclare's analysis of women coming for alcoholism treatment (Sclare, 1970) found that their help-seeking was triggered by either 'employment' or 'domestic' stress.

The risk of increasing employment stress amongst women will have risen with the increasing number of women being employed. Moreover, some women have entered occupations and acquired positions known to be particularly stressful where they experience the demands of decision-making, responsibility, competition, and career pressures which were once virtually a male monopoly.

Not only might more women be experiencing these pressures, but they will in many cases have to cope with these stresses in addition to their other responsibilities as housewives and mothers. The dual pressure of holding down a job and maintaining home and family can create intolerable pressures for some women, and the tranquillizing and relieving effect of alcohol is one recourse they may take. Indeed, a recent American survey found that women in non-traditional or multiple roles were more likely to drink than women with purely domestic responsibilities (Keil, 1978).

It is pertinent then to refer back briefly to the Treasury Report (Information Division, 1974), for this shows that the major increase in women's employment has been amongst married women. This analysis of changes in women's employment over the fifty years from 1921-71 reported that whereas in 1921 only 10 per cent of young married women were employed, in 1971 nearly half the married women under thirty were and 'the 1971 figures show a continual increase in the economic activity of married women between the ages of 30 and 50' (Information Division, 1974: 2). It is also interesting to note that American epidemiologists (Bailey, Haberman, and Alksne, 1965: 2) attributed the higher alcohol consumption and incidence of problem drinking amongst Negro women compared to white women not only to the more permissive drinking culture of Negroes whose bars were populated roughly equally by men and women, but also to the fact that a much higher proportion of black women than white women were employed, and were heads of one parent families. Thus their multiple roles were particularly exacting but economic importance greater. The same nexus of social and economic responsibilities, which puts Negro women at more risk than white women, is now coming to apply more to women in general.

It has also been shown that even amongst normal drinkers, female motivations for drinking are much more likely than males to be for 'escape' reasons (Schuckit, 1972). Women tend to report putting more value on the psychotropic effects of alcohol as a mood changer, tranquillizer, and psychological and physical anaesthetic. If women drink more than men to experience a sense of escape from difficult situations and if there is amongst women a greater feeling that there is more to escape

from, then given the increasing availability of alcohol it is not surprising that more women should be drinking and getting into problems as a result. A similarity can be traced here with the massive
increase amongst women in the uses of other legal tranquillizers
and sleeping aids such as Mogadon, Valium, and Librium.

(ii) SPECIFIC LIFE EVENTS

Sclare's second basis of stress amongst women problem
drinkers – 'domestic stress' – can also be conjectured to have
been increasing in prevalence, not just in the generally increasing
pressures on women with dual roles, but more importantly with
the increasing incidence of specific stressful situations. Beckman
(1975: 799) concluded from her reviews of various studies that
'alcoholism and heavy drinking in women appear more likely to
be linked to psychological stress and a specific precipitating
circumstantial situation than is alcoholism or heavy drinking in
men'. One study (Lisansky, 1957) found that twice as many
women as men cited a specific past experience (e.g. an unhappy
love affair, the death of a parent or spouse, divorce) as the point
when they started off drinking heavily. Lolli (1953) reported that
women alcoholic patients were more likely than alcoholic men to
have been moderate consumers until they had been confronted
with some difficult situation. If, then, as we know, more women
are drinking heavily and experiencing problems, we might
conjecture therefore that an increasing number of women may
have been faced with a greater number of stressful 'specific
precipitating circumstantial situations'.

In their seminal work on life events that triggered depression,
Brown and Harris (1978) have consistently returned to the
concept of 'loss' as the predominant feature of the precipitating
triggers of depression. 'Loss' might be through the death of a
loved one, through children leaving home, even through moving
house and losing old habits and surroundings. The concept of
'loss' also appears important in recurring etiological triggers
found amongst women with drinking problems – notably the loss
of fertility and/or children, particularly in middle age, and the
loss of a relationship through divorce or separation.

Curlee (1969, 1970) has suggested that about 20 per cent of
women problem drinkers started mis-using alcohol at the time of

a middle-age identity crisis, precipitated by some situational event, although it has been suspected that her sample might have over-represented middle-aged, middle-class female alcoholics. Indeed, Curlee (1969) has traced particularly the relationship of onset of heavy drinking amongst women to the 'empty-nest syndrome', which occurs when children grow up and leave home. For many women this can be exacerbated by menopausal difficulties and the realization of how much they rely on their role in the family as mother and wife for their identity and for feelings of worth and purposefulness; the loss of fertility combined with children leaving the domestic scene can produce a sense of pointlessness and feelings of no longer being needed. These factors will be discussed more thoroughly later in this book by Wilson (chapter 5).

It would of course be difficult to assert definitely that this sort of situation is becoming more common for women, but taking a long retrospective view, it is reasonable to suggest that more women are likely to experience these situations now than they were twenty or thirty years ago, because of the post-war trend in our social structure away from the three generation family towards the two generation structure, a move reflected and reinforced by housing policies, and greater geographical occupational mobility, and which may encourage more adolescents and young married couples to leave the parents' home.

It is less contentious to relate the increasing prevalence of drinking problems to the growing fragmentation of marital relationships, as evidenced by the increasing incidence of separation and divorce. Over the years, very many studies have reported a high incidence of divorced and separated women amongst populations of alcoholics, and one review has put this figure as comprising between a third and two thirds of all women diagnosed as alcoholics (Schuckit, 1972). A study of 524 alcoholics treated in many different agencies (Moss and Beresford Davies, 1967) showed that there were six times as many divorces amongst female alcoholics as there were amongst women in the general population. The correlation between divorce and alcoholism is something of a chicken and egg relationship in that it is not always possible to determine which of the two is the more important cause of the other. In many cases an increasingly difficult marital or emotional relationship and tendency towards excessive drinking invariably interact and aggravate each other in a deteriorating vicious circle. Nevertheless, because of the evidence implicating stressful life events as important triggers in the onset of psychiatric and drinking difficulties amongst women, there is a good reason for believing that in many cases, the breakdown of a relationship can be meaningfully implicated as precipitating drinking problems amongst women. Thus a rising divorce rate could be regarded as yet another indicator of increasing social disruption facing women in modern society and as another cause of situations that have made women increasingly likely to develop drinking problems. And indeed *Table 10* below shows that between 1966 and 1976 in the UK, both the rate of divorces per head of the married population, and the actual numbers of decrees granted, more than trebled.

Table 10   *Divorces in selected years in England and Wales, 1966-1976*

year	rate per 1,000 of married population	numbers granted of decrees nisi and decrees absolute
1966	3·2	78,565
1967	3·5	86,606
1969	4·1	104,214
1971	6·0	162,126
1973	8·4	211,721
1975	9·6	240,062
1976	10·1	256,526

Source: Office of Population Censuses and Surveys, Lord Chancellor's Dept.
Condensed from *Annual Abstract of Statistics* (1978), HMSO.

(iii) ROLE AMBIGUITY

A common thread runs through all the foregoing description of life events and situations known to increase the risk of women drinking excessively, be it the menopause, children leaving home, or failure in an emotional relationship – they are all threats to the woman's image of herself in feminine roles – as mother, home maker, wife, and lover.

'Although alternative interpretations of some of the events are possible, many of them can be viewed as posing acute threats to a woman's sense of feminine adequacy. In particular, divorces, separations, and other marital problems and reproductive difficulties would seem likely to arouse doubts in most women about their adequacy or worth as women'. (Wilsnack, 1973: 77)

A husband's death or children leaving home may also cause feelings of worthlessness in women if the roles of wife and mother have been central aspects of her self image and if her husband or children have been important reinforcers of her femininity.

Of course, many women experience the sort of problems cited above without becoming excessive drinkers. Rather it is those women who feel threats to feminine adequacy most acutely who are at most risk of developing drinking problems.

'Most studies of female alcoholics either imply or state explicitly that alcoholic women have problems in the area of feminine identification. Such terms as "role confusion", "masculine identification", "poor feminine identification", and "inadequate adjustment to the adult, female role" occur frequently in clinical studies of alcoholic women.' (Wilsnack, 1973: 67).

The assumption has often been made that women who drank excessively were somehow more manly than other women, because they were indulging in behaviour more common amongst men, and because early psychoanalytic theories related alcoholism to homosexuality (Curlee, 1967). However, all the evidence from research studies points to the finding that 'alcoholic women do not reject femininity and the female role, but tend, if anything, to over emphasize and over value the female role. Positive attitudes towards the female role, toward femininity and motherhood are confirmed from several sources' (Gomberg, 1976: 143). The difference is that alcoholic women express more concern than other women about their *inability* to perform traditional motherly and wifely roles and about their *failure* to maintain viable relationships (Kinsey, 1966). In short then there is a strong relationship between a woman's uncertainty about her adequacy in female roles which she consciously values, and the development of a drinking problem. Unrealistic hyper-femininity combined with a sense of failure in achieving womanliness leads to feelings of frustration and anger which are acted out in excessive drinking (Bardwick, 1971). Gomberg (1976) has noted that women take alcohol as an escape from unresolvable conflicts, and Pemberton (1967) showed that women often drank heavily to relieve feelings of being unable to fulfil a satisfactory role within the family unit.

The relevance of all this to the rising prevalence of drinking problems amongst women is that these studies suggest it would be mistaken to interpret the increase in women's drinking primarily as a manifestation of assertiveness and pseudomasculinity. Rather, it may be an attempt to recoup a declining sense of womanliness.

For it can certainly be argued that, over recent years, women have become more likely to experience role confusion and feelings of unfulfilled achievement. At one time, prevailing social attitudes maintained that it was normal for a woman to be a housewife, that it was natural for her to be passive, demure, and emotionally warm, and that her most fulfilling achievement was to give birth. But as these ideologies have become increasingly questioned, the role of housewife and mother is now often referred to as dull, imprisoning, and demeaning. Even if all women do not accept this view, doubts must have been raised in many a mind. Furthermore, the feminist lobby have tended to lead instead towards male criteria of success and achievement through obtaining status, acclaim, or high earnings. Roles adopted in a woman's working life can be discrepant with the traditional stereotype of women as non-competitive. So the present position is an ambiguous one, with the retention of old ideologies against the 'career woman' as being somehow hard and unfeminine. There is also still some disapproval of women working full-time when they have young children. Indeed it seems that whatever a woman's role, there will be some doubt about its appropriateness. The value placed on any woman's social and sexual roles has become increasingly uncertain. Behaviours and roles that were once universally seen as natural and fulfilling are now implicated as the ideological values of a sexist society, whilst those same ideologies are still strong enough to undermine any new roles and behaviours for women. The upshot is an era of ambiguity and uncertainty for women, which is most disquieting of all for those women who have doubts about their womanliness and experience particularly acute sex-role identification problems. Moreover the irony of 'emancipation' is that many women have widened their visions of what they might be able to achieve and a more flexible view of how they could behave, and yet feel that in reality these alternatives are still denied them or are too difficult to obtain. Thus what were once non-problematic roles have become seen as valueless, but these have only been replaced by the promise of expectations that are continually unfulfilled – unrealistic expectations which are continually raised, only, in most cases, to be dashed. It would not therefore be surprising if over recent years, more women had come to feel the frustrations that are known clinically to trigger women towards heavier drinking. Jesser, Carman, and Grossman (1968) found that the lower the expectation of having ones needs for achievement satisfied, then the greater would be the recourse to alcohol, and this was especially true amongst the women subjects in the study.

(iv) SOCIOSEXUAL SELF-IMAGE

However, the tension women have increasingly come to experience between established stereotypes and more flexible interpretations has perhaps become most acute in the area of sexual attitudes and behaviour, and it is in this area where studies such as those of Kinsey (1966) and Parker (1972) have also found the most acute identity problems of women problem drinkers. The role of woman as careful and passive in sexual encounters has gradually become redundant because of increasing control of fertility. Women have become allowed to be more sexually aggressive and explicit, to make the play, and to have as much right to orgasm, greater choice of partner, and enjoyment of sex as men. But as yet, this too has been a highly ambivalent development which is by no means unanimously agreed behaviour. Sexual emancipation, like other aspects of emancipation has again only served as yet to increase the sex role confusions which have been found etiologically to precipitate drinking problems amongst women (Lisansky, 1957; Wilsnack, 1973). Double standards still prevail. It is still fairly positive for a man and definitely negative for a woman to be promiscuous; the differential valuation of the 'stud' and the 'scrubber' remain strong. (Similarly, recent survey evidence (Shaw *et al.*, 1978) has found that the highly negative view of drunkenness amongst women compared to its relative tolerance amongst men is just as strong a difference as it has always been). Despite women's greater freedom to indulge in casual sex and to drink more, women still experience guilt about doing either, and for many of them, the opportunity to indulge in these more flexible behaviours has only manifested itself paradoxically, like the myth of equality of opportunity, as an increasing source of frustration. The 'sexual revolution' has merely raised doubts in women about their adequacy as sex objects and sexual performers. The current preoccupation with obtaining orgasm, assertiveness, and the demands that women must enjoy sex has raised doubts and uncertainties in many women's minds about their sexual adequacies, and their feelings of ambivalence have become intensified. Women who at one time may have been relatively satisfied with their sexual relationships now feel unfulfilled if their experiences do not live up to the propaganda of liberated women's magazines. Again this will not be a universal problem for all women, but given that problem drinking amongst women is triggered by sex-role problems and identity problems, and is highly concentrated amongst women who feel sexually inadequate and frigid – albeit in some cases with promiscuity, which is not necessarily discrepant – it is very likely that the changing climate of sexual mores has put more women at greater risk of turning to alcohol as a recourse.

In these senses, the increasing prevalence of alcoholic women is not so much the ransom of emancipation as rather the paradoxical and ironical outcome of a nascent social trend which must attack old attitudes and open up new horizons, but in doing so increases sex role ambiguity, double standards, confusion and guilt, and aggravates women's feelings of not being able to realize their potential.

Vulnerability and protection factors

We have discussed many reasons why women have changed their

drinking habits over recent years and increased their alcohol consumption. But we must now go on to consider the left hand side of our original etiological diagram. For we cannot explain a rise in prevalence simply in terms of women's alcohol consumption catching up with men's, since surveys have shown that groups whose drinking patterns are identical still differ in the number of alcohol problems they report, because of different levels of vulnerability to, or protection from, experiencing drinking problems (Cartwright, Shaw, and Spratley, 1978). We must ask, then, in what ways women are more vulnerable to drinking problems than men, and in what ways they are more protected, and go on to consider whether there has been any change in this balance, although as our etiological diagram implies, the set of factors causing changes in drinking habits are also the same range of factors that affect the balance of vulnerability and protection. Thus we have already considered various aspects of female vulnerability to drinking problems – their reaction to stressful life events for example – and possible reasons why sources of this vulnerability may have become more prevalent. Indeed in discussing female vulnerability, it is clear that psychological and physical factors are the most pertinent.

Psychological and physical vulnerability factors

The case can certainly be made that women are more vulnerable generally to psychological difficulties than are men, and this may make groups of women who drink the same amount in relatively the same way as men more likely to get into psychological difficulties because of their drinking.

It has always been the case that women have outnumbered men in mental hospital admissions, as psychiatric out-patient clinic attenders, and in help-seeking for psychological problems, especially neuroses (Gomberg, 1976). Neither is this just because, as might be argued, that women are simply more likely to seek or receive such help, because survey studies of psychopathological symptoms have also found that mental disorder is two to three times as prevalent amongst women as men (Hare and Shaw, 1965; Shepherd *et al.*, 1966).

All this might have important implications for their vulnerability to psychological problems over alcohol dependence, especially as women appear to drink less for social reasons than men, and more for the psychotropic effects of alcohol (Orford, Waller and Peto, 1974; Knupfer and Room, 1964).

There is more conclusive evidence of women's greater physiological vulnerability to alcohol. This material will be outlined in more detail in the next two chapters, but for now it can be noted that it takes less alcohol, consumed over fewer years to cause liver damage amongst women than men and that women exhibit much more physical illness in association with alcoholism than do men (Wilkinson, *et al.*, 1969). The reasons for this are presumed to be that, on average, the physiological effects of alcohol are much greater on women, because of their generally smaller body size, and because a man's body contains 5 per cent to 10 per cent more water than a woman's, so that alcohol becomes more diluted in their system (Bell, Davidson, and Scarborough, 1968). The result of this, of course, is that the same amount of alcohol tends to have greater toxic effect on women's bodily organs, and women, on average, achieve higher blood alcohol levels than men from the same amount of alcohol. It is also thought that women's greater bodily vulnerability to alcohol may be aggravated at times by menstrual and menopausal difficulties (Jones and Jones, 1976).

The net result of women's higher psychological and physiological vulnerability is that they combine to produce a 'telescoped' prognosis, i.e. there is a much shorter time between early problem drinking and the development of severe symtomology amongst women than men. Women applying for alcoholism treatment tend to have much shorter histories of heavy drinking than male patients (Curlee, 1970; Sclare, 1970; Wilkinson, Santamaria, and Rankin, 1969).

Vulnerability factors and the acceleration of prevalence

In themselves these factors of greater vulnerability do not explain a *rise* in the prevalence of drinking problems amongst women. However, they *do* help to explain why the rise has become more rapid than male prevalence. Since all the factors we have discussed have been creating a greater likelihood that women's consumption of alcohol on average will have increased, then given their greater risk of developing physiological and psychological problems than men from a given level of alcohol consumption, this will mean that the female rate of alcohol-related diseases and problems will *accelerate* more than men's and produce higher prevalence rates than would be expected from the increase in consumption alone. In effect, the greater acceleration of the prevalence of drinking problems amongst women is created by the same factors which make the development of drinking problems amongst individual women more telescoped than amongst men. This would explain the findings in surveys that the more alcoholics there are in any particular sub-group of the population, the higher will be the proportion of female alcoholics in that group. As the number of alcoholics go up, the number of female alcoholics has been found to increase more rapidly than the number of males (Haberman and Sheinberg, 1967).

PROTECTION FACTORS

In previous eras, women's greater physical and psychological vulnerability to drinking problems has been offset by higher sociological protection. Whilst women seem to be more vulnerable to internalized, neurotic conditions, men have tended to be more vulnerable to personality disorders, and deviancy of a more sociopathic type. Thus, whilst women have outnumbered men in terms of mental illness, men have always outnumbered women in the commital of crime. Because of the taboos against acting out and antisocial behaviour amongst women, they have tended not to get involved in sociopathic behaviour. The prevalence statistics at the beginning of this chapter demonstrated this. Drunkenness offences (*Table 1*) are the most obviously sociopathic index there is and women are sociologically protected against either committing, being arrested or convicted for, drunkenness. Hence this index had the greatest ratio of males to females. However, in those areas where women were more vulnerable than men – on liver cirrhosis mortality for example (*Table 4*) – the male and female rates were almost identical despite the lower average consumption by women.

What those statistics (*Tables 1, 2, and 4*) indicated was that those protective factors which used to make it less likely that women would experience the more sociopathic types of alcohol problems are becoming eroded. For the male/female ratio on drunkenness arrests has been shrinking and this reflects not just a rise in consumption amongst women, but also the easing of taboos against women drinking, drinking in groups, and drinking in public. It also reflects a general trend towards more sociopathic behaviour amongst women. Crime in general has been increasing amongst women. As *Table 11* demonstrates, indictable crimes (i.e. 'serious' offences such as theft and murder) have been increasing at a faster rate amongst women than amongst men; whilst since 1973, the number of non-indictable crimes (i.e. less 'serious' crimes such as vagrancy and traffic offences) have been falling amongst men but increasing amongst women.

Table 11 *Persons found guilty of indictable and non-indictable offences in England and Wales in selected years, 1969-1977.*

year	indictable offences in thousands			non-indictable offences in thousands			total M:F ratio
	males	females	M:F ratio	males	females	M:F ratio	
1969	264·5	39·6	6·7:1	1203·7	98·9	12·2:1	10·6:1
1971	277·3	44·5	6·2:1	1260·7	105·5	12·0:1	10·3:1
1973	292·3	45·2	6·5:1	1465·4	125·8	11·7:1	10·3:1
1975	342·1	60·4	5·7:1	1456·8	129·5	11·3:1	9·5:1
1977	360·8	67·9	5·3:1	1431·9	141·5	10·1:1	8·6:1

Source: Home Office. Condensed from *Annual Abstract of Statistics* (1978), HMSO.

The erosion of the protective factors which used to apply against women developing drinking problems is part of the general ransom of emancipation. Emancipation means greater freedom, and greater freedom means less protection. Thus to the old adage that 'men get drunk and women get depressed', should now perhaps be added 'men get drunk and women get depressed and drunk'.

It would appear then that the increasing prevalence of drinking problems amongst women is but part of a sea change in their roles in society, their attitudes to themselves, their behaviour, and their self identity. The pervasive shift away from traditional feminine roles into more ambiguous territory has created a situation where women's former values are questioned, but the propriety of newer behaviours and multiple roles have not been established or accepted without guilt. The encouragement for women to become more assertive and demonstrative has resulted in an increasing incidence of female roles and behaviour that bring about internal dissension and uncertainty. When combined in some cases with the greater practical stresses of carrying out multiple roles in the family and society at large, and inexperience in dealing with the greater amount of personal economic freedom, it is little wonder that women's behaviour and attitudes regarding drink and drinking behaviour should have begun to move in a manner consistent with all these trends and pressures.

Increasing prevalence amongst young women

There is a further qualifying emphasis to be added to this picture, which is that the stresses of multiple roles, role ambiguity, greater economic independence, and more sociopathic behaviour – all factors predisposing modern women towards greater alcohol consumption and greater numbers of drinking problems – have all concentrated especially amongst younger women.

Consider, for example, the question of higher economic independence for women. The average man's income is at its highest between the ages of thirty and fifty, but according to the New Earnings Survey of 1977, (Annual Abstract of Statistics, 1978) a woman's income is now actually at its highest between the ages of twenty five and twenty nine. The Department of Employment has also pointed out (Information Division of the Treasury, 1974: 2) that more women under thirty are now employed because 'In the past it was usual for a woman to leave work when she married. Now it is more usual for her to stay at work until the first child is due.' Given the rise in economic power of younger women, it is hardly surprising that advertisers have aimed drink sale campaigns particularly at younger women, and that brewers and publicans have designed and refurbished public houses to attract their clientele (*Financial Times*, 1976).

It is also this same group who are most subject to the tensions over roles, sexual mores, and self identity discussed earlier, and who are particularly subject to crises over gynaecological problems, abortions, and divorces, thus triggering a pattern of seeking recourse in the psychotropic effects of alcohol. In 1976, for example, 46, 366 women divorced were aged under thirty (Annual Abstract of Statistics, 1978).

This higher concentration of etiological pressures on young women again has its most obvious manifestation in the rates of drunkenness offences, for as *Figure 2* below shows, in 1970-76, the most dramatic rises in female drunkenness offences occurred in the age group eighteen to twenty-one, and the number of female offenders aged between twenty-two and under thirty began to surpass the number of offences made by all the women aged between thirty-one and sixty.

Looking back still further one finds that the prevalence of

Figure 2   Female drunkenness convictions by age group, 1970-76

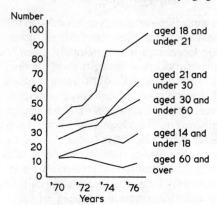

Source: Condensed from Home Office (1977).

female drunkenness between 1961 and 1975 actually decreased amongst women sixty and over, and only increased by a third amongst women aged thirty-one to sixty, but it increased three times amongst the aged twenty-two to thirty group, and four times amongst the eighteen to twenty-one group.

Future trends

What then can be said of the future? Although today's young women will eventually become tomorrow's middle-aged women and may reduce their risk of experiencing drinking problems as perhaps less of them become employed, or they socialize less in clubs and public houses, nevertheless in many other ways they will carry through with them the new permissive drinking norms. Moreover they will carry these permissive views about drinking into those times of their life when they might be faced with the stress of menopause and their children leaving home. Furthermore, a rising cohort of women as yet young or unborn, will come to adopt the risks and the values of our changing and increasingly permissive culture as regards female behaviour. If social and economic trends continue in their current direction then we can certainly expect the prevalence of drinking problems amongst women to continue to rise.

From the general etiological overview presented in this chapter it should be clear that much more is involved in the rising number of women problem drinkers than the mere increase in consumption. Indeed, the reasons for, and effects of, that increase are themselves manifold. And still more is involved – the whole gamut of changes in social expectations, pressures, and practicalities affecting modern women. Therefore, no-one should be deluded into believing that banning drink advertisements or banning alcohol from supermarkets will be preventive cure-alls. What society decides to do about women's problem drinking, or how it affects it, is in many ways out of the control of the alcohologist, the medical and social services, and health planners. But what is within the grasp of these bodies to achieve now is a reorientation of their approach and views about women drinkers, and a realization that the old methods focusing exclusively on the problem of alcohol consumption or alcohol dependence will be even more misleading and one-sided in the treatment and recognition of alcohol problems amongst women, than it has been in men. Indeed, if there is a message from the rise in prevalence of drinking problems amongst women, it is that the causes of this increase are so manifold, that they are essentially rooted in the whole experience of being a woman in modern society.

References

Accept (1977). *Second Annual Report*, London.

Alcoholics Anonymous (1972) *Findings of the UK Survey.* London: AA General Service Board Mimeo.

Alliance News (1975) *More Women Join AA.* May/June: 14. London: UK Temperance Alliance Ltd.

____ (1976) *Women Drink more Wine, less Tea.* Nov/Dec: 19. London: UK Temperance Alliance Ltd.

____ (1977) *Vermouth Sales more than Doubled.* Jan/Feb: 11. London: UK Temperance Alliance Ltd.

Annual Abstract of Statistics (1978) London: HMSO.

Bailey, M.B., Haberman, P.W., and Alksne, M.A. (1965) Epidemiology of Alcoholism in an Urban Residential Area. *Quarterly Journal of Studies on Alcohol 26*:19-46.

Bardwick, J.M. (1971) *Psychology of Women.* New York: Harper and Row.

Beckman, L.J. (1975) Women Alcoholics: A Review of Social and Psychological Studies. *Quarterly Journal of Studies on Alcohol 36*: 797-824.

Bell, C.H., Davidson, J.N., and Scarborough, K. (1968) *Textbook of Physiology and Biochemistry.* Baltimore: Williams and Wilkins.

Brewers' Society (1978) *UK Statistical Handbook.* London: Brewing Publications Ltd.

Brown, G. and Harris, I. (1978) *The Social Origins of Depression.* London: Tavistock.

Cahalan, D., Cisin, I.H., and Crossley, H.M. (1969) *American Drinking Practices.* New Haven, Conn: College and University Press.

Cartwright, A.K.J. and Shaw, S.J. (1978) Trends in the Epidemiology of Alcoholism. *Psychological Medicine* **8**: 1-4.

Cartwright, A.K.J., Shaw, S.J., and Spratley, T.A. (1978) The Relationship between Per Capita Consumption, Drinking Patterns and Alcohol Related Problems in a Population Sample, 1965-1974. *British Journal of Addiction.* **73**: 237-258.

Christian Economic and Social Research Foundation (1978) *Twenty-Fifth Annual Report. Chief Constables' Reports, England and Wales, and Scotland 1977. Part One Drink*

Offences London: Publications of the Christian Economic and Social Research Foundation.

Curlee, J. (1967) Alcoholic Women. *Bulletin Menninger Clinic* *31*: 154-163.

_____ (1969) Alcoholism and the Empty Nest. *Bulletin Menninger Clinic* **33**: 165-171.

_____ (1970) A Comparison of Male and Female Patients at an Alcoholism Treatment Center. *Journal of Psychology 74*: 239-47.

De Lint, J. and Schmidt, W. (1971) Consumption Averages and Alcoholism Prevalence: a Brief Review of Epidemiological Investigations. *British Journal of Addiction 72*: 237-246.

Duffy, J.C. (1977) Estimating the Proportion of Heavy Drinkers. In D.L. Davies (ed.), *The Ledermann Curve: Report of a Symposium*. London: Alcohol Education Centre Publications.

Edwards, G., Hensman, R.C., Hawker, A., and Williamson, V. (1967) Alcoholics Anonymous: The Anatomy of a Self-Help Group. *Social Psychiatry* **1**:4

Edwards, G., Hensman, R.C., and Peto, J. (1972) Drinking in a London Suburb III. Comparisons of Drinking Troubles among Men and Women. *Quarterly Journal of Studies on Alcohol*. Supplement No. 6: 120-128.

Financial Times (1976) Monday March 29, p. 1.

Gomberg, E.S. (1976) Alcoholism in Women. In B. Kissin and H. Beigleiter (eds), *The Biology of Alcoholism Vol. 4. Social Aspects of Alcoholism*. New York: Plenum.

Haberman, P.W. and Sheinberg, J. (1967) Implicative Drinking reported in a Household Survey: A Corroborative Note on Subgroup Differences. *Quarterly Journal of Studies on Alcohol 28*: 538-593.

Hare, E.H. and Shaw, G.K. (1965) *Mental Health in a New Housing Estate*. Maudsley Monograph 12. London: Oxford University Press.

Home Office (1972) *Report of Department Committee on Liquor Licensing*. Cmnd. 5154. London: HMSO

_____ (1977) *Offences of Drunkenness 1976 in England and Wales*. Cmnd. 6952. London: HMSO.

Homes and Gardens (1978) December issue.

Information Division of the Treasury (1974) *Progress Report*. No. 56, November. London.

Jesser, R., Carman, R.S., and Grossman, P.H. (1968) Expectations of Need Satisfaction and Drinking Patterns of College Students. *Quarterly Journal of Studies on Alcohol 3*: 465.

Jones, B. and Jones, M. (1976) Intoxication, Metabolism and the Menstrual Cycle. In M. Blatt and M.A. Schukit (eds), *Alcoholism – Problems in Women and Children*. New York: Grune and Stratton.

Keil, J.T. (1978) Sex-role Variations and Women's Drinking: Results from a Household Survey in Pennsylvania. *Quarterly Journal of Studies on Alcoholism 39*: 859-867.

Kinsey, B.A. (1966) *The Female Alcoholic: a Social Psychological Study*. Springfield, Illinois: Thomas.

Knupfer, G. and Room, R. (1964) Age, Sex, and Social Class as Factors in amount of Drinking in a Metropolitan Community. *Social Problems 12*: 224.

Lawrence, J.J. and Maxwell, M.A. (1962) Drinking and Socio-economic Status. In O.J. Pittman and C.R. Snyder (eds), *Society, Culture and drinking patterns*. New York: Wiley.

Lisansky, E.S. (1957) Alcoholism in Women; Social and Psychological Concomitants. I. Social History Data. *Quarterly Journal of Studies on Alcoholism 18*: 588-623.

Lolli, G. (1953) Alcoholism in Women. *Connecticut Review of Alcoholism 5*: 9-11.

Makela, K. (1975) Consumption Level and Cultural Drinking Patterns as Determinants of Alcohol Problems. *Journal of Drug Issues 5*: 344.

Massot, P., Hamel, D., and Deliry, P. (1956) Alcoolisme feminin, donnes statistiques et psychopathologiques. *Journal of Medicine 37*: 265-269. Lyon.

Miller, C.H. and Agnew, N. (1974) The Ledermann Model of Alcohol Consumption. Description, Implications and Assessment. *Quarterly Journal of Studies on Alcoholism 35*: 877-898.

Moss, M.C. and Beresford-Davies, E. (1967) *A Survey of Alcoholism in an English County*. London: Geigy Scientific Publications.

National Council on Alcoholism (1979) *NCA News 5*. London.

National Council of Women (1976) *Report of a Working Party on Alcohol Problems in Women and Young People*. London: National Council of Women.

Orford, J., Waller, S., and Peto, J. (1974) Drinking Behaviour and Attitudes and the Correlates among University Students in England. *Quarterly Journal of Studies on Alcoholism* **35**(4): 1316-74.

Otto, S. (1977) Women, Alcohol and Work. In M. Grant and W.H. Kenyon (eds) *Alcoholism and Industry*. London: Alcohol Education Centre Publications.

Parker, F.B. (1972) Sex-role Adjustment in Women Alcoholics. *Quarterly Journal of Studies on Alcoholism 33*: 647.

Pemberton, P.A. (1967) A Comparison of Outcome of Treatment in Female and Male Alcoholics. *British Journal of Psychiatry 113*: 367.

Ratcliffe, M. (1979) Catch a Woman Customer. *Supermarketing*. March 30, 6 & 7.

Riley, J.W. and Marden, C.F. (1947) The Social Pattern of Alcoholic Drinking. *Quarterly Journal of Studies on Alcoholism 8*: 265.

Robinson, D. (1979) *Talking Out of Alcoholism*. London: Croom Helm Ltd.

Room, R. (1972) Drinking Patterns in large US Cities: a Comparison of San Francisco and National samples. *Quarterly Journal of Studies on Alcoholism*, Supplement. *6*: 28-57.

Schuckit, M. (1972) The Woman Alcoholic. *Psychiatry in Medicine 3*: 37.

Sclare, A.B. (1970) The Female Alcoholic. *British Journal of Addiction 65*: 99-107.

Shaw, S.J., Cartwright, A.K.J., Spratley, T.A., and Harwin, J. (1978) *Responding to Drinking Problems*. London: Croom Helm Ltd.

Shepherd, M., Cooper, B., Brown, A.C., and Walton, G.W. (1966) *Psychiatric Illness in General Practice*. London: Oxford University Press.

Somerset Council on Alcoholism (1975) *Annual Report*. Taunton, Somerset.

Sulkunen, L. (1976) Drinking Patterns and the Level of Alcohol Consumption: an International Overview. In R.J. Gibbins (ed.), *Research Advances in drug and alcohol problems*. Vol. 3. New York: Wiley.

Whitehead, P.C. and Ferrence, R.G. (1976) Women and Children Last: Implications of Trends in Consumption for Women and Young People. In M. Greenblatt and M.A. Schuckit (eds), *Alcohol Problems in Women and Children*. New York: Grune and Stratton.

Wilkinson, P., Santamaria, J.N., Rankin J.G., and Martin, D. (1969) Epidemiology of Alcoholism: Social Data and Drinking Patterns of a Sample of Australian Alcoholics. *Medical Journal of Australia 1*: 1020-1025.

Wilkinson, P., Santamaria, J.N., and Rankin J.G. (1969) Epidemiology of Alcoholic Cirrhosis. *Australian Annals of Medicine 18*: 222-226.

Wilsnack, S.C. (1973) The Needs of the Female Drinker: Dependency, Power, or What? *Proceedings of 2nd Annual Conference*: 65-83. National Institute on Alcohol Abuse and Alcoholism.

Wilson, C. (1976) Women and Alcohol. Paper presented at USA Air Force in Europe School. London: *Camberwell, Council on Alcoholism paper*.

2

A. HAMID GHODSE

Consultant Psychiatrist
St. George's Hospital, Tooting, London

G. S. TREGENZA

Assistant Psychiatrist
St. George's Hospital, Tooting, London

The physical effects and metabolism of alcohol

The main therapeutic uses of alcohol throughout its long history have been as an analgesic and as a surgical anaesthetic. The discovery of the process of distillation by the Persian physician, Rhazes (c. 900 A.D.) was, however, a turning point in its use, as it then became possible to produce beverages of much greater potency. These distilled liquors were originally used medicinally rather than recreationally, and alcohol was believed to be the 'elixir of life' with extraordinary powers of healing.

In addition, alcohol is the oldest documented substance of abuse; reports describing its disabling effects date back to the ancient civilizations of Egypt and Mesopotamia, and by the first century B.C., alcoholism had been recognized in Rome.

Despite this long history, the pharmacological effects of alcohol have been investigated only comparatively recently. Most studies have been carried out on the male population and scant attention has been devoted to any differences between the sexes as far as the effects of alcohol are concerned. Some of the reasons for this comparative lack of interest in the effect of alcohol on women are documented in other chapters. In this chapter some of the general effects of alcohol are described, and where information is available, the specific effects of alcohol on women are discussed even if the evidence is only scanty.

The word 'alcohol' is loosely used to refer to ethyl alcohol which is the intoxicating ingredient of alcoholic beverages. It is a member of a group of compounds that are chemically related, although some, such as methyl alcohol ('meths'), are highly poisonous.

Pure ethyl alcohol is a clear, colourless liquid with a weak odour and a burning taste. It is produced by fermentation of various sugars by yeast fungi. Subsequent distillation processes are utilized to increase the alcohol concentration of a fermented brew.

Alcoholic beverages consist mainly of ethyl alcohol and water with added congeners (other alcohols) to give characteristic colour and flavour to different beverages. The pharmacological action, if any, of congeners is not certain but they are thought to increase the intoxicating effects and hangovers.

Absorption, distribution, and excretion

When taken orally, alcohol is readily absorbed into the blood stream from the small intestine. The rate of absorption is slower from diluted beverages such as beer, and other factors such as food or anxiety may retard absorption. An approximate intake of 4-5 pints of beer (1 gram per kilogram of body weight – the average female body weight being 60 kilogrammes, male 70 kilogrammes) will produce maximum blood level (100 milligrammes per cent) after one hour, so that the person would experience intoxication. The concentration of alcohol in blood is easily measured and is usually a good estimate of the concentration throughout the water content of the body. It can usefully be regarded as one objective measure of intoxication; but intoxication does depend on the way in which the body 'handles' alcohol, i.e. the interaction of the processes of absorption, distribution, and elimination.

From the blood stream alcohol is rapidly and uniformly distributed throughout the body water and there appears to be no specific areas that selectively store alcohol. It easily crosses the placenta into the foetal circulation and also passes into the milk of lactating women.

Most of the alcohol consumed is eliminated from the body by metabolism in the liver. Enzymes convert it to intermediate metabolites and ultimately to its simple chemical components of carbon dioxide and water. Only a small proportion (2-10 per cent) of an alcohol dose is excreted unaltered via the lungs, the kidneys, and the skin. The average rate of elimination in humans is about 100 milligrammes alcohol per kilogram of body weight per hour, i.e. the alcohol in a four oz whisky would take five to six hours to disappear entirely from the blood stream of an average sized person.

Recent studies have shown some significant differences in the handling of alcohol by men and women, and this is probably related to the finding that young females have a substantially lower proportion (50 per cent) of their total body weight in the form of water than have young men (60 per cent) (Bell, Davidson, and Scarborough, 1968).

In standardized conditions in one study (Jones and Jones, 1976) subjects consumed doses of alcohol which had been individually calculated on the basis of body weight. Blood alcohol levels were measured at intervals after consumption and the results analysed statistically. Maximum blood levels were reached sooner in the women indicating a more rapid rate of absorption. Their peak alcohol levels were also consistently and significantly higher, which is in accordance with the concept of alcohol diffusion into a proportionately smaller pool of body water.

It was also found that the peak alcohol levels attained by the males were generally quite constant from test to test, whereas the females showed a considerable variability of response, dependent, it seemed, on the stage of the menstrual cycle at which the test was undertaken. The levels were found to be higher during the premenstrual and ovulatory phases.

Alcohol metabolism in women was, in general, faster than in men, thus although the women became more intoxicated than the men (i.e. they had higher peak blood alcohol levels), they did not remain intoxicated for longer. Women on oral contraceptives, however, metabolised alcohol significantly more slowly but more regularly and predictably (Jones and Jones, 1976).

The implications of these findings are as yet speculative, but the researchers have suggested that the greater variability and unpredictability of response to alcohol by females may make them more cautious when drinking and this may lead to a slower rate of development of alcohol tolerance in women. In other words, if women do drink more cautiously than men, their physiological processes are exposed to less alcohol and therefore have less opportunity to get used to its effects.

Glucose metabolism

Alcohol consumption can cause hypoglycaemia or hyperglycaemia. In lay terms, this means that alcohol can cause either low or high levels of sugar in the blood. In medical terms, hypoglycaemia results from a reduction of both gluconeogenesis and of the conversion of glycogen to glucose and is particularly likely to occur in young children or undernourished subjects; even small amounts of alcohol may therefore be dangerous if consumed by these groups. The mechanism of alcoholic hyperglycaemia is not fully understood, but the release of catecholamines from the adrenal medulla by alcohol and impaired peripheral uptake of utilization of glucose are probably contributory factors.

Gastrointestinal tract

Alcohol in moderate amounts stimulates the flow of saliva and stomach secretions, but high concentrations are inhibitory. As it is an effective stimulus for gastric acid secretion, alcohol is inadvisable for patients with peptic ulcers.

High concentrations of alcohol are irritating to the stomach mucosal lining and cause inflammation and erosions. About one third of heavy drinkers suffer from chronic gastritis and abnormalities of the oesophagus and duodenum also occur; carcinoma of the oesophagus has increased prevalence among alcoholics (Schmidt and De Lint, 1972; Adelstein and White, 1976).

Moderate amounts of alcohol do not significantly impair the digestion of food but, because of its effect on gastsric functioning, high doses can delay absorption and cause vomiting.

The pancreas is quite sensitive to heavy regular alcohol intake, and acute or chronic pancreatitis may occur. Impaired pancreatic function may account for the poor absorption of dietary fats and fat soluble vitamins in alcoholics, leading to states of malnutrition and vitamin deficiencies (Ritchie, 1975).

Cirrhosis is probably the best known complication of alcoholism, although the majority of alcoholics do not develop cirrhosis. It is a disease in which permanent structural damage to the liver occurs and which has a high mortality rate. Changes in its incidence reliably reflect changes in the average alcohol consumption in the population, but it is, in fact, not the only form of liver disease attributable to the toxic effects of alcohol.

Fatty liver, due to abnormal deposition of fat, probably occurs in the majority of alcoholics. It is generally a benign condition which is reversible on abstention from alcohol, but fatal complications have been reported, particularly among negro women (Kramer, Juller, and Fisher, 1968).

Alcoholic hepatitis has been said to occur in up to 30 per cent of heavy drinkers and to have a mortality of 10-30 per cent (Galambos, 1972; Hardison and Lee, 1966). Although the conditions are distinct, susceptibility to cirrhosis seems to be increased in those who have previously suffered from alcoholic hepatitis.

Severe liver disease usually follows years of heavy drinking, although a moderate alcohol intake sometimes results in cirrhosis. 'Binge' drinking seems to be less harmful to the liver than steady, regular drinking (Brunt *et al.*, 1974).

Various studies have been published that indicate that being a female is in itself a significant predisposing factor in the development of alcohol-related liver disease. Wilkinson *et al.* (1971) in Australia have reported that women alcoholics are more predisposed than men to cirrhosis, and Williams and Davis (1977) have found that a markedly higher proportion of the women patients in the liver unit of a London hospital had the most serious forms of liver damage. The difference in the male-female incidence of severe disease was significant in patients aged less than forty-five, but not significant in those over the age of fifty-five, although the women had histories of alcohol intake strikingly lower than that of the men. Follow-up showed a more gloomy prognosis for females: they were more likely to progress from alcoholic hepatitis to cirrhosis, less likely to respond favourably to abstention from alcohol, and died at a younger age than males. Quite why pre-menopausal women should be particularly vulnerable to the hepatotoxic effects of alcohol is not clear, but with the increasing numbers of female heavy drinkers, the findings of these studies may be of a similarly increasing significance.

Central nervous system

The effect of alcohol on the brain and central nervous system is, of course, the reason for its widespread consumption. Contrary to popular belief, its action is predominantly depressant or sedative. The apparent stimulant effect is due to depression of natural inhibitory mechanisms. With increasing blood levels, the relatively less susceptible excitatory functions of the brain become depressed, leading ultimately to stupor and coma.

Alcohol impairs various sensory, perceptual, mental, and motor functions. The most highly integrated functions are affected first, with resultant disorganization of thought and bodily inco-ordination. Concentration, memory, judgment, and insight are clouded. Mood changes, emotional outbursts, and impulsive acts often occur. In general, mental or physical abilities are not enhanced by alcohol but moderate amounts may improve skilled performance in a person who is affected by severe anxiety. However, attention and reaction time are adversely affected and the importance of alcohol in causing road accidents is well known.

Chronic alcohol ingestion can cause a variety of psychotic states and neurological disorders. Polyneuritis, Wernicke's encephalopathy, Korsakoff's psychosis, dementia, 'blackouts', and alcohol hallucinations may occur.

Recently, there has been growing evidence that chronic alcoholism may be associated with cerebral atrophy and brain damage detectable by computerized axial tomography (EMI scanning) and psychological tests, in the absence of overt clinical signs (Lishman, Ron, and Acker, 1980). There is also evidence of increased susceptibility to alcohol-related brain damage in women (Wilkinson *et al.*, 1971). This is an area that needs further research.

The nervous system is also sensitive to abrupt abstention from alcohol by those who are physically dependent upon it and a withdrawal syndrome ensues, characterised by tremor, which may vary from slight trembling to severe shaking. Insomnia frequently occurs and in severe instances, delirium tremens, with gross tremor, illusions, delusions, and hallucinations may develop. Grand mal convulsions are another life-threatening complication. The alcohol withdrawal syndrome is similar to that induced by other central nervous depressants such as barbiturates and benzodiazepines which can be used to treat the symptoms of alcohol withdrawal.

Cardiovascular function

Moderate doses of alcohol increase the blood flow to the body surface leading to flushing and a feeling of warmth. However, increased sweating and depression of the temperature regulating mechanism may cause a fall in internal body temperature. The pulse rate may be increased, as may the blood pressure, although this is a long-term consequence of excessive alcohol consumption.

The prevention of anginal pain that sometimes occurs with moderate blood alcohol levels is probably due to depression of pain centres within the brain, as there is no evidence of improved flow within the coronary arteries and, in fact, high doses of alcohol slightly reduce the blood flow in the coronary circulation. In contrast, blood flow to the brain is increased by high blood alcohol levels.

A specific form of damage to the heart muscle (alcoholic heart muscle disease) can occur as a consequence of chronic alcohol abuse and may be a cause of congestive heart failure and death in alcoholics (*British Medical Journal*, 1979).

Interaction with other drugs

As a central nervous system depressant itself, alcohol potentiates the action of other sedative drugs. The combination of alcohol with any such drug (e.g. sleeping tablets, tranquillizers, narcotics, anti-depressants, and antihistamines) is potentially dangerous and sometimes lethal.

Prolonged heavy alcohol consumption causes increased

metabolism of some drugs, notably those used for the treatment of epilepsy, for some types of diabetes, and for thrombosis. Acute intoxication with alcohol may inhibit the metabolism of the same drugs. The clinical consequences of either effect may be considerable.

Interference with the metabolism of alcohol by disulfiram ('Antabuse') leads to an accumulation of aldehyde in the blood stream and causes nausea, headache, and a fall in blood pressure. The drug is sometimes used in the treatment of alcoholics but, on occasion, if the patient does drink, the reaction can be dangerous. Metronidazole ('Flagyl') which is frequently used to treat some vaginal infections and oral hypoglycaemic agents may also cause a similar, though generally weaker, reaction.

Many other drugs may be dangerous in people with liver disease, such as alcoholic cirrhosis.

Endocrine system and sexual function

The interaction of alcohol and hormones is particularly complicated in the context of human sexual behaviour. It seems likely that alcohol may have very different effects on the sexual functions of men and women, although most research on the effect of alcohol on the endocrine system and sexual behaviour involves only males, as though only males drink alcohol and only males have sexual interests. With the dearth of knowledge about the effects of alcohol on women, one can only make the most tentative speculations based on research carried out on men. For this reason, some effects of alcohol on men are included.

The acute consumption of alcohol affects various vital glands. For the more physiologically-minded catecholamines are released from the adrenal medulla and there is also an increase in serum cortisol levels. The latter effect is thought to be mediated via the hypothalamus and anterior pituitary, as it does not occur in hypophysectomized animals. Growth hormone levels are also increased after alcohol ingestion, but antidiuretic hormone (ADH) and oxytocin, which are both secreted from the posterior pituitary, are suppressed.

Quite common in male alcoholics is atrophy of the testicles, impaired sexual drive and fertility. It has been suggested that this has been due to failure of the alcoholic liver to metabolize oestrogens or more directly to the action of alcohol on the hormones important to maintaining health of sexual organs. Chronic, heavy consumption of alcohol slows the motility of sperm, changes their structure, and probably reduces fertility.

In terms of its acute effects, alcohol is popularly considered an aphrodisiac. Although it increases sexual desire by reducing the inhibitions of the cerebral cortex, it also impairs performance. In women as in men, sexual behaviour is governed by a complex interaction of psychological and physiological factors and is thus controlled by the central nervous system and both divisions of the autonomic nervous system (i.e. the sympathetic and parasympathetic divisions). The effect of alcohol on sexual activity is likewise complicated and there has been inadequate study of the effects of alcohol on women's sexuality. It is possible that a reduction of central inhibition and anxiety by alcohol may increase sexual arousal. In addition, it has been observed that alcoholic women tend to have a greater number of miscarriages than non-alcoholics. This could be due to a higher conception rate which, in turn, could be attributed to a lack of contraceptive measures or, as has been suggested, although there is no substantiating evidence, may be a reflection of greater sexual activity.

Alcohol is also noted to inhibit contraction of the uterus during childbirth and lactation so that, ironically, attempts to dislodge an unwanted pregnancy by means of a hot bath and a bottle of gin generally do not succeed. Adverse effects of alcohol consumption during pregnancy are discussed in the next chapter.

Menstrual cycle

Female physiological functioning and female psychology are patently interrelated. Premenstrual tension can vary from mild mood change to severe depression and emotional lability, and is associated, for example, with an increased suicide rate. Transient depression after childbirth is very common ('the baby blues') and the postpartum period is also associated with the onset of serious mental illness in some women. The menopause, too, is well known to be a time of widely variable psychological upset as well as physical changes. The affective disturbances that occur in relation to the menstrual cycle, childbirth, and the menopause are probably a consequence of the combination of both psychodynamic factors and physiological factors such as fluctuating hormone levels. Whether female alcoholism may sometimes be specifically related to female physiology has been the focus of a number of studies, but the results have been conflicting.

Wall (1937) and Lolli (1953) postulated a direct relationship and suggested that premenstrual tension underlies the cyclic nature of some women's drinking. Another study concluded there was no simple correlation between alcoholism and premenstrual tension (Lisansky, 1957).

In a study of women alcoholics and the menstrual cycle, Podolsky (1963) felt that the women who drank more during the premenstrual phase did so to ease the symptoms of premenstrual tension which in itself symbolized the woman's acceptance of her sex role and her ability to cope with external stresses and interpersonal relationships.

Belfer and Shader (1976) studied a group of thirty-four alcoholic women and the majority related their drinking to the menstrual cycle and, in particular, to the premenstrual phase. For these women there was no overt disturbance of menstrual or sexual function, nor a correlation with the severity of premenstrual symptoms.

Using various standard psychological tests, they also found that the alcoholic women, whether they related their drinking to the menstrual cycle or not, were found to be significantly more depressed than a control group. They also found that their ratings on a femininity scale were 'normal', although previous anecdotal studies had suggested disturbances in feminity in women alcoholics. None of the tests shed any light on unconscious disturbances in sexual identity.

Because of its dependence to a large extent on anecdotal material and the shortage of objective measurable data, this area of study is wide open to differing interpretations and conclusions. Nonetheless, with these shortcomings borne in mind, an approach that takes account of the interacting physiological and psychological factors of the individual, is likely to be useful in increasing knowledge of both the aetiology and effective treatment of problematic drinking in at least some women.

Conclusion

Throughout this chapter it has been apparent that there is a great shortage of accurate information on the physical effects and metabolism of alcohol in women. Indeed, most work refers to 'alcoholics' and often fails to mention the sex of subjects; it is assumed that alcoholics are male. However, with the increasing number of alcohol-related problems in women, it is becoming more important to know accurately any specific areas of susceptibility. For example, it has already been shown that women who drink alcohol excessively and develop liver disease, are more likely to suffer serious harm. Undoubtedly, further significant differences between male and female alcoholics will be found in future as further research is carried out in this previously unexplored area.

References

Adelstein, A. and White, G. (1976) Alcoholism and Mortality. *Population Trends 6*: 7-13. London: HMSO.

Belfer, M. and Shader, R. (1976) Premenstrual Factors as Determinants of Alcoholism in Women. In M. Greenblatt and M.A. Schuckit (eds), *Alcoholism Problems in Women and Children*. New York: Grune and Stratton.

Bell, C.H., Davidson, J.N., and Scarborough, H. (1968) *Textbook of Physiology and Biochemistry*. Baltimore: Williams and Wilkins.

British Medical Journal (1979) Alcoholic Heart Muscle Disease. *British Medical Journal 2*: 1457-58.

Brunt, P.W., Kew, M.C., Scheuer, P.J., and Sherlock, S. (1974) Studies in Alcoholic Liver Disease in Britain. I. Clinical and Pathological Patterns related to Natural History. *Gut*: 15-52.

Galambos, J.T. (1972) *Alcoholic Hepatitis: its Therapy and Prognosis*. In J. Popper and F. Schaffner (eds), *Progress in Liver Diseases* Vol. IV. New York: Grune and Stratton.

Hardison, W.G. and Lee, F.I. (1966) Prognosis in Acute Liver

Disease of the Alcoholic Patient. *New England Journal of Medicine* **275**: 61.

Jones, B. and Jones, M. (1976) Intoxication, Metabolism and the Menstrual Cycle. In M. Greenblatt and M.A. Schuckit (eds), *Alcoholism Problems in Women and Children*. New York: Grune and Stratton.

Kramer, K., Juller, L., and Fisher, R. (1968) The Increasing Mortality Attributed to Cirrhosis and Fatty Liver in Baltimore (1957-66). *Annals of Internal Medicine:* 69-273.

Lisansky, E. (1957) Alcoholism in Women: Social and Physiological Concomitants. *Quarterly Journal of Studies on Alcohol* **18**: 588-623.

Lishman, W.A., Ron, M., and Acker, W. (1980) Computed Tomography and Psychometric Assessment of Alcoholic Patients. To appear in D. Richter (ed.) Addiction and Brain Damage. London: Croom Helm.

Lolli, G. (1953) Alcoholism in Women. *Connecticut Review on Alcoholism*: 9-11.

Podolsky, E. (1963) The Woman Alcoholic and Premenstrual Tension. *Journal of the American Medical Womens Association* **18**: 816-818.

Ritchie, M. (1975) The Aliphatic Alcoholic. In L.S. Goodman and A. Gilman (eds), *The Pharmacological Basis of Therapeutics*. 5th Edition. New York: Macmillan.

Schmidt, W. and de Lint, J. (1972) Causes of Death of Alcoholics. *Quarterly Journal of Studies on Alcohol* **33**: 171-185.

Wall, J. (1937) A study of Alcoholism in Women. *American Journal of Psychiatry* **93**: 943-952.

Wilkinson, P., Kornaczewski, A., Rankin, J.G., and Santamaria, J.N. (1971) Physical Disease in Alcoholism. Initial Survey of 1,000 patients. *Medical Journal of Australia* **1**: 1217-1223.

Williams, R. and Davis, M. (1977) Alcoholic Liver Diseases – Basic Pathology and Clinical Variants. In G. Edwards and M. Grant (eds), *Alcoholism: New Knowledge and New Responses*. London: Croom Helm.

3

ASTOR BALFOUR SCLARE

Consultant Psychiatrist
Duke Street Hospital, Glasgow

The foetal alcohol syndrome

A century ago little attention was paid to risk factors during pregnancy. To a large extent such non-recognition of hazards in pregnancy was of course due to lack of scientific knowledge regarding the vulnerability of the unborn child. It is only in recent years that we have gained precise information as to how the foetus may be affected by a variety of physical insults occurring during the early stages of the mother's pregnancy.

The observations of Gregg in Australia in 1941 drew attention to the potentially deleterious effect upon the foetus of maternal rubella (German measles) during early pregnancy. Later the risk of harm caused to the embryo by other viruses such as herpes virus hominis and cytomegalovirus became known to the medical profession. For some time of course there had been medical concern about the possible transmission of maternal syphilis to the foetus. The occurrence of the thalidomide disaster in 1961, with its emphasis upon limb deformities and other abnormalities in the infants of mothers who had taken this hypnotic drug in early pregnancy, served further to heighten public awareness of the medical hazards run by pregnant women. Moreover, the medical profession has thereafter been continuously concerned with the possible teratogenic effects of drugs. The Committee on Safety of Medicines now insists upon the necessity for new drugs to pass stringent teratogenicity tests, among other things, before being approved for therapeutic use.

During the past decade there has been a marked increase in the number of foetal disorders diagnosed antenatally by the technique of amniocentesis. Increasing emphasis is now being placed on genetic counselling prior to embarking on a pregnancy.

In the late 1960s reports became available regarding the occurrence of heroin dependence in the newborn infants of women who were abusing heroin during pregnancy. The factor of drug intake in relation to neonatal problems was thus further highlighted. During the 1970s we have gained new information indicating that heavy cigarette smoking in early pregnancy tends to be associated with 'small for dates' infants at birth. Antenatal care programmes now give attention to pregnancy risk factors such as virus diseases, therapeutic drug intake, and cigarette consumption. Furthermore, the possible damage to the foetus caused by X-rays of the mother's abdomen during early pregnancy is now well known.

As indicated, the growth of scientific knowledge about the role of various environmental stress factors in pregnancy has provided a major contribution to the new public and medical consciousness of the hazards of childbearing. The vast change which has taken place in the social role of women during the past 100 years has also played a part in bringing about new attitudes towards pregnancy. In mid-Victorian times many working-class women had numerous pregnancies; their maternal responsibilities were limited only by the relatively high infant mortality rate at the time. At the turn of this century it was commonplace for women in this country, and in others, to spend a substantial proportion of their lives in the pregnant state and in the care of young children. Not surprisingly, many perceived themselves masochistically as little else than baby-producing machines.

The suffragette movement, the contribution of Marie Stopes, the women's liberation movement, the *Sex Discrimination Act* (1975), and, above all, new-found means of fertility control, especially the contraceptive pill, have permitted women in general to re-evaluate their role in society and to regard themselves with a fresh dignity. Choice in regard to pregnancy is now possible and comparatively easy. This psychosocial change affecting feminine status allows a more positive attitude towards pregnancy, an attitude which has been encouraged in recent years by women's magazines. The Natural Childbirth Trust has further served to emphasize the joys of childbearing. Women themselves have now begun to take a considerable interest in the hazards of pregnancy and their possible avoidance. A Private Member's Bill, although unsuccessful, was submitted in 1976 to restrict the prescribing rights of doctors. It did at least express public and professional concern over adverse reactions to drugs.

Earlier concern about alcohol intake in pregnancy

Although the possible adverse effect on the unborn child or a pregnant woman's consumption of alcohol has recently attracted considerable attention in medical circles, awareness of this danger is by no means new. In the Book of Judges (13.3) the angel of the Lord says to a childless woman, 'You are barren and have no child, but you shall conceive and give birth to a son. Now you must do as I say: be careful to drink no wine or strong drink'. Drs Jones and Smith in their 1973 article on the subject make reference to the regulation in ancient Carthage that bridal couples were forbidden to drink on their wedding night in order to prevent the conception of defective children. In 1834 a Select Committee investigating the serious problem of alcohol abuse at that time declared that the infants of alcoholic mothers may have 'a starved, shrivelled and imperfect look'. This observation was more impressionistic than scientific, but is nevertheless of some interest. In 1900 Dr W.C. Sullivan, working in the women's prison in Liverpool, commented upon the high incidence of abortion and stillbirth among alcoholic women and also upon the high rate of epilepsy among their surviving offspring. Again, such observations did not apparently spring from a rigorous scientific investivation but they probably have some validity. East (1936) indulged in some useful speculation as to whether alcohol could cause either genetic damage or damage to the foetus 'in utero'.

Animal experimentation

In the field of medical science, experiments on animals can

sometimes provide important pointers towards the mechanism of disease production. Admittedly it cannot always be assumed that the way in which a disease is brought about in animals is necessarily a precise replica of a similar disease process in the human being. Moreover, the experimental laboratory conditions employed in the production of morbid processes in research animals may differ drastically from those governing human illness. The time scale of laboratory-induced disease may also be shorter than that which occurs in the case of human pathological conditions. Laboratory-provoked cancer in mice may be to a large extent comprehensible in terms of the particular genetic strain of mouse and its known susceptibility to malignant disease. Interpretations must be cautious. Nevertheless, bearing such reservations in mind, it can be readily asserted that animal models of disease have on many occasions illuminated the human situation.

An early experiment by Nice in 1912 suggested that alcohol produced increased fertility but a higher rate of infant mortality in white mice than in control animals. Later work by Stockard and Papanicolaou in 1918, this time studying the progeny of guinea pigs which had been rendered alcoholics, indicated that smaller litters were produced. Perhaps this contrary result could to some extent be explained by species differences (white mice and guinea pigs) – a well known trap in the comprehension of animal experiments. On the other hand, Durham and Woods in 1932 failed to replicate the findings of Stockard and Papanicolaou in guinea pigs. Such contrary results are not infrequently achieved in laboratory research and can usually be traced to differences in experimental strategy. Certainly the history of experimentally induced damage resulting from alcohol in animals contains some baffling and contrary conclusions. On the other hand, the finding of increased intrauterine deaths and of diminished size and weight of offspring by Stockard and Papanicolaou in the descendants of alcoholic guinea pigs seems to be almost non-controversial and, as will be seen later, of some possible relevance to the human situation.

In 1927 a careful study by MacDowell and Lord – reverting to mouse experimentation – showed a raised intrauterine death rate among animals exposed to alcohol vapour. An experiment using rats instead of mice (Davenport, 1932) concluded that alcohol exposure led to smaller litters and that the offspring had diminished learning capacity compared with control animals. Laale in 1971 found that the offspring of zebra fish exposed to alcohol displayed congenital malformations.

Turning finally to more recent laboratory work: the experiment of Tze and Lee in 1975 utilized Sprague-Dawley female rats to whom ethanol was given as their only fluid for five weeks prior to mating and also during pregnancy. Valid control groups of rats, not given alcohol, were set up. When compared with the control groups, the alcohol-fed rats produced offspring which were smaller in size and number than those of the control rats. This effect could not be attributed to differences in calorie intake between the groups. Of some possible relevance to the human problem of the foetal alcohol syndrome is the fact that Tze and Lee's infants of alcohol-fed rats were not only reduced in body size but showed a disproportionately diminished head circumference, dry skin, and generally shrivelled appearance. Such work represents an amplification of Davenport's 1932 study. Tittmar in 1977, in a carefully contrived experiment with Wistar rats, confirmed the specific effect of alcohol upon birth weight of the offspring of alcohol-fed animals but no congenital defects were observed.

The field of animal experiment is to some extent confusing. Contrary findings may be explained by species susceptibility, nutritional factors, and methodological differences, e.g. is alcohol given orally or intravenously to the laboratory animal and at which stage of pregnancy? Although there is a real danger of facile extrapolation of animal data to humans, laboratory experiments have tended to indicate that alcohol given to certain pregnant animals may lead to reduction in the size and number of their offspring and possibly also to development defects.

The foetal alcohol syndrome in humans

During the past decade a certain amount of evidence has become available that the ingestion of considerable amounts of alcohol by pregnant women may lead to a particular pattern of maldevelopment in their infants. To be sure, this state of affairs, if it is finally verified, would confirm and extend some of the conclusions deriving from the animal work described above. However, a degree of uncertainty remains as to the existence and specificity of this condition in human infants. Such uncertainty has not deterred some individuals with a sense of evangelical purpose from engaging in petulant political campaigns for instantaneous governmental action regarding this hazard.

Many would agree that we cannot as yet be conclusive in our view as to whether alcohol causes a specific form of damage to the unborn child. Experts who undertake research into congenital abnormalities in infants admit to frequent difficulty in pinpointing the cause of such malformations. Moreover, if alcohol is indeed a significant teratogen, we do not know what quantity of alcohol taken over what period of time by a pregnant woman is likely to have a deleterious effect upon the foetus.

The first indication of this clinical problem in modern times was presented by Borteyru (1967) in France, a nation with a serious alcohol problem. A year later Lemoine and his colleagues in France published details of what still remains the largest series of cases of the so-called foetal alcohol syndrome. They described details of 127 cases of infants in whom there were abnormalities of the face and head, mental handicap, and diminished stature. In some instances, the mother, and in others the father, of the child was noted to be alcoholic.

At first, little attention was paid in Britain to these findings. However, a series of reports from the Dysmorphology Unit in Seattle, USA in the 1970s (Jones and Smith, 1973; Jones *et al.*, 1973; Jones *et al.*, 1974), appearing in the British medical press, served to highlight the topic here. Nevertheless medical interest in the matter has kindled very slowly. The present writer referred to the subject in his address in London to the annual general meeting of the Medical Council on Alcoholism in 1975.

Scepticism and caution continue to characterize professional attitudes at present to the problem of the foetal alcohol syndrome. To some extent this conservatism is appropriate, especially when one bears in mind the difficulty of isolating alcohol as the sole or principal causal factor operating in such cases. However, an excessively negative attitude towards the almost certain existence of this infantile defect will have the unfortunate effect of inhibiting research, and will not establish the true prevalence of the syndrome and the attendant degree of risk associated with pregnancy in the drinking woman.

Dr Christy Ulleland (1970), an instructor in paediatrics at

Harborview Hospital in Seattle, was among the first to embark upon an epidemiological approach to the question of possible effects upon the foetus of the female alcoholic. He found that among 1600 babies born at the hospital during an eighteen-month period, twelve were born to mothers who could be defined as alcoholic. Of these twelve infants, ten were found to be underdeveloped. By contrast, only thirty-seven of the remaining 1588 babies born to non-alcoholic women were underdeveloped. Accordingly it seemed that having an alcoholic mother enormously increased the chance of a newborn infant being underdeveloped. Of the twelve infants whose mothers were considered to be alcoholic, eight failed to 'catch up' in their expected increase in weight and indeed four failed to grow substantially even after admission to hospital for special feeding and care. Five of the infants born to alcoholic mothers displayed retarded brain development on special tests.

This study which looked at the problem as it occurred within a defined population represented a landmark in the acquisition of knowledge. Some query, however, could be raised about this particular population which was heavily slanted towards lower socioeconomic groups. Could the infantile abnormalities be attributable as much to maternal undernutrition, heavy smoking, and other sociomedical factors as to alcohol ingestion?

Further investigations undertaken in the Dysmorphology Unit in the Department of Paediatrics at Seattle (Jones *et al.*, 1973 and 1974) served to inculcate alcohol more convincingly as an important causal agent in producing malformations in newborn babies. These were reported in the medical press in the early 1970s. By this time it became possible to establish a more clear-cut description of the catalogue of defects that could occur in the foetal alcohol syndrome. It was also becoming acknowledged that considerable variation in the severity and pattern of the congenital malformations could occur. Such variability no doubt stems from differences in the quantity and frequency of alcohol consumption by the pregnant woman at different stages of gestation – thus affecting to different degrees the development of different organs. By 1976 Hanson, Jones and Smith were able to report a total of forty-one cases of foetal alcohol syndrome (FAS) in the Seattle research. Clarren and Smith (1978) were later able to summarize the clinical findings in 245 cases. What are the essential features of this condition? They are the following:-

(1) *Growth Deficiency*. This would seem to be the most characteristic feature. Unlike many other 'small for dates' babies at birth, the impairment of growth is of girth more than length. Thus the FAS infant appears undersized and 'linear'. S/he fails to show 'catch-up' growth in the first few months of life. S/he may come to medical attention in the first place simply through such failure to thrive. His/her parents may, for instance, complain that they are unable to 'fatten him/her up'. His/her body is in fact likely to have less than the normal complement of fatty tissue.

(2) *Abnormalities of the Head and Face*. The FAS infant has a cranium of abnormally small circumference. This condition of microcephaly reflects impaired development of the brain, possibly as a direct influence of alcohol during embryonic life. The face also usually manifests abnormalities. The palpebral fissure of the eye is shortened; the upper lip is underdeveloped. Shortsightedness and squints often occur. There is commonly a short, retroussé nose and a flattened profile. In some cases, cleft palate and hare lip are observed. The individual facial anomalies are subtle and perhaps unimpressive as single features. The whole facial 'set', however, is rather typical and forms a strong pointer to the diagnosis of FAS.

(3) *Brain Deficiency*. Mental handicap is noted in the majority of cases. This tragic effect is unquestionably due to failure of brain development 'in utero' as a result of circulating alcohol. Streissguth and her colleagues (1978) have reported a mean IQ of sixty-five in twenty FAS patients of varying ages. Another outcome of the central nervous system deficiency is the occurrence of fractiousness, tremulousness and feeble sucking responses in FAS babies. Moreover, hyperactivity in these children is frequent and may possibly arise from the brain defect.

(4) *Associated Features*. Various organs may be affected. Abnormal development of the heart may, for instance, take place, resulting in defects such as atrial or ventricular septal defect. The external genitals may be maldeveloped and a kidney abnormality, hydronephrosis, may sometimes occur. Limited movement of the joints of the fingers and elbows, and abnormal crease patterns in the palm of the hand, may be observed. Haemangiomas ('birth marks') may be seen on the skin.

Recognition of the foetal alcohol syndrome

Can the FAS be readily identified in an infant or child? As mentioned previously, it is not always easy to distinguish the pattern of one congenital malformation from another, especially when a newborn infant is observed to have a confusing multiplicity of defects. Infants with FAS may superficially resemble those with the de Lange or Noonan syndromes. Again they may have some features in common with rare conditions such as trisomy – eighteen familial blepharophimosis or the Smith-Lemli-Opitz syndrome.

However, the history of the pregnant alcoholic, as well as that of heavy drinking during the early stages of pregnancy, should serve as strong pointers. The pattern of growth deficiency, craniofacial abnormalities, brain deficiency, and associated features in the infant, coupled with such a history in the mother, should then place the diagnostician on surer ground. Nevertheless, the identification of the syndrome seems to be more unequivocally regarded in the United States at present. Some diagnostic hesitancy persists in Britain.

Unfortunately few types of mental handicap can be identified prior to birth. Perhaps at some future date it may become possible through special diagnostic techniques to recognize the FAS before birth.

Mechanism of the foetal alcohol syndrome

At the present time we have no certain knowledge as to precisely how the damage is brought about in infants with FAS. It is not even clear as to whether the pathological mechanism is mediated principally through the mother or father of the unborn child. The report of Lemoine and his colleagues (1968) from France refers to a number of cases of FAS in which the father rather than the mother had an alcohol problem. This information suggests an affection of the paternal germ plasm prior to or about the time of fertilization.

On the other hand, the teratogenic process may operate through the mother. Possibly different variants of FAS are produced by different mechanisms. As Woollam (1978) points out, ethanol may affect the mother by lowering the level of glucose or oxygen in the blood. This would be a plausible mechanism as the developing tissues of the foetal brain are likely to be particularly sensitive to a lack of glucose or oxygen. However, the main action of alcohol may be exerted upon the placenta, upon the umbilical circulation or more directly upon the cells of the developing foetus. Another possibility may be that a breakdown product of ethanol, e.g. acetaldehyde, rather than ethanol itself, may be responsible for the damage to the foetus. The experiments of Woollam's team at Cambridge, using acetaldehyde as an experimental agent with rats, certainly suggest that their offspring can develop a FAS-like condition with this substance.

As yet we do not know if the use of certain drugs, e.g. tranquillizers, in association with alcohol may have an especially damaging effect upon the foetus. Nor is there clear information yet as to the quantity of alcohol or type of drinking pattern, e.g. 'binge' drinking or sustained consumption, which may be specifically pathogenic. Further research is likely to provide answers to such questions.

Treatment and prevention

In considering the therapeutic aspects of the FAS problem, attention requires of course to be paid to both mother and child. The task on both fronts is a formidable one. So far as the mother is concerned, the Seattle workers are firmly of the opinion that the FAS is now such a well-defined form of malformation, and such a tragic occurrence, that termination of pregnancy should be offered to women who are diagnosed as alcoholic and who have been imbibing substantial amounts of alcohol during the early stages of pregnancy. It is during this early phase that the central nervous system of the embryo is being formed. Certainly the comparatively liberal *Abortion Act* 1967 (in the United Kingdom) presents no clinical or legislative barrier to therapeutic interruption of a pregnancy that carries a substantial risk of alcohol-induced damage to the unborn child. At the end of the day, however, the wishes and attitudes of the pregnant woman herself must constitute a major factor in any such clinical decision-making. In the meantime, it would seem that obstetricians would do well to add alcohol to the already considerable number of teratogenic risk factors.

Quite apart from the emergency issue of therapeutic abortion in the case of suspected FAS, there arises an important question of learning to identify and treat alcoholism in women of child-bearing age. The recognition of alcohol abuse in women is not always a simple matter as this behaviour often takes place in a lonely, non-sociable, clandestine, guilt-ridden manner at home. However, increasing awareness of the problem on the part of family doctors should be of assistance, provided that due attention is paid to this subject at our medical schools, especially during courses in psychiatry, community medicine, and general practice.

To date the topic of alcoholism has attracted all too little teaching time for the medical undergraduate and many doctors have come to regard it as not forming part of 'real medicine'. The Medical Council on Alcoholism, by conducting symposia in recent years for medical students, has gone some way towards filling the gap. However, faculties of medicine in our universities still require to take appropriate action if sufficient information about women alcoholics and the FAS are to be communicated.

Other professionals such as health visitors and social workers also require to obtain similar knowledge during basic training and in refresher courses. Indeed, in general terms, the meagre health content in social work training leaves a great deal to be desired.

So far as pregnant women themselves are concerned, clear information must be conveyed to them about the risks of heavy drinking in regard to the wellbeing of the foetus. It is possible that even moderate drinking may be hazardous. The French investigation of Kaminski *et al.* (1976) suggested that more serious abnormalities may occur in the infants of mothers who consume beer rather than wine. Family doctors, obstetricians, midwives, and health visitors themselves need to be in possession of the relevant facts if they are to convey them to their patients.

Further research

The features of the FAS seem to have been fairly well-defined mainly through American and French research. There has been no substantial British contribution to this work. The time is now ripe for a medical investigation of this problem in the United Kingdom. Probably the most fruitful line of enquiry would be to identify a cohort of women alcoholics of reproductive age and to examine retrospectively their childbearing history and their offspring in detail as well as prospectively to study their obstetric history and progeny. Careful neuropathological examination of any deceased infants of such mothers could also be revealing. A region such as Scotland, with its high prevalence of alcoholism, would probably prove to be rewarding for a study of this nature.

Conclusion

A substantial body of evidence from clinical sources and animal experimentation has now accumulated to suggest that a characteristic set of physical and mental defects, known as the foetal alcohol syndrome (FAS), may occur in the infants of alcoholic mothers. The precise incidence and the underlying mechanism are not fully understood yet. In the meantime it would be reasonable to advocate that alcohol abuse in early pregnancy be widely regarded as hazardous by patients and doctors alike.

References

Borteyru, J.P. (1967) La toxicomanie alcoölique parentale et ses repercussions sur la descendance. Thèse: Université de Nantes.

Clarren, S.K. and Smith, D.W. (1978) The Foetal Alcohol Syndrome. *New England Medical Journal* **298**: 1063-67.

Davenport, C.B. (1932) Effects of Alcohol in Animal Offspring. In H. Emerson (ed), *Alcohol and Man*. New York: Macmillan.

Durham, F.M. and Woods, H.M. (1932) Alcohol and Inheritance: An Experimental Study. *Medical Research Council Special Report Series No. 168*. HMSO: London.

East, W.N. (1936) *Medical Aspects of Crime*. London: Churchill.

Gregg, N.M. (1941) Congenital Cataract following German

Measles in the Mother. *Transactions of the Ophthalmological Society of Australia* 3: 35-46.

Hanson, J.W., Jones, K.L., and Smith, D.W. (1976) Foetal Alcohol Syndrome: Experience with 41 patients. *Journal of the American Medical Association* 235: 1458-60.

Jones, K.L. and Smith, D.W. (1973) Recognition of the Foetal Alcohol Syndrome in Early Infancy. *Lancet* 2: 999-1001.

Jones, K.L., Smith, D.W., Ulleland, C.N., and Streissguth, A.P. (1973) Pattern of Malformation in Offspring of Chronic Alcoholic Women. *Lancet* 1: 1267-71.

Jones, K.L., Smith, D.W., Streissguth, A.P., and Myrianthopoulos, N.C. (1974) Outcome in Offspring of Chronic Alcoholic Women. *Lancet* 1: 1076-1078.

Kaminski, M., Rumeau-Rouquette, C., and Schwartz, D. (1976) Consummation d'alcool chez les femmes enceintes et issue de la grossesse. *Revue d'Epidémiologie et de Santé Publique* 24: 27-40.

Laale, H.W. (1971) Ethanol Induced Notochord and Spinal Cord Duplications in the Embryo of the Zebrafish Brachydanio Rerio. *Journal of Experimental Zoology* 177: 51.

Lemoine, P., Harousseau, H., Borteyru, J.P., and Menuet, J.C. (1968) Children of Alcoholic Parents: Anomalies Observed in 127 Cases. *Quest Medical* 25: 476-482.

MacDowell, E.C. and Lord, E.M. (1927) Reproduction in Alcoholic Mice, 1. Treated Females. A Study of the Influence of Alcohol on Ovarian Activity, Pre-natal Mortality and Sex Ratio. *Archiv. für Entwicklungsmechanik der Organismen* 109: 549-83.

Nice, L.B. (1912) Comparative Studies of the Effect of Alcohol, Nicotine, Tobacco and Caffeine on White Mice. *Journal of Experimental Zoology* 12: 133.

Select Committee (1834) *Report on Drunkenness*. House of Commons. London.

Stockard, C.R. and Papanicolaou, G.N. (1918) Further Studies on the Modification of the Germ Cells in Mammals: the Effect of Alcohol on Treated Guinea Pigs and their Descendants. *Journal of Experimental Zoology* 26: 119.

Streissguth, A.P., Herman, C.S., and Smith, D.W. (1978) Intelligence, Behaviour and Dysmorphogenesis in the Foetal Alcohol Syndrome. *Journal of Paediatrics* 92: 363-67.

Sullivan, W.C. (1900) The Children of the Female Drunkard. *Medical Temperance Review* 1: 72-79.

Tittmar, H.G. (1977) Some Effects of Ethanol, Presented during the Prenatal Period, on the Development of Rats. *British Journal on Alcohol and Alcoholism* 12: 71-83.

Tze, W.J. and Lee, M. (1975) Adverse Effects of Maternal Alcohol Consumption on Pregnancy and Foetal Growth in Rats. *Nature* 257: 479-80.

Ulleland, C.N. (1972) The Offspring of Alcoholic Mothers. *Annals of the New York Academy of Sciences* 197: 167-69.

Woollam, D. (1978) *The Foetal Alcohol Syndrome*. Paper read at conference on Alcohol and the Family, 18 February 1978. Birmingham: United Kingdom Alliance.

4

Senior Lecturer/Director
Alcohol Studies Centre
Paisley College, Scotland

Psychological aspects of women and alcohol

Introduction

Any consideration of the psychological aspects of women and alcohol must commence with the repetition of the well-established fact that drinking alcohol is predominantly a male behaviour. Drinking habit surveys clearly show that when compared to females of their own age, social class, and ethnicity, males drink more alcohol, more frequently, and this alcohol is usually consumed in male company. For example, in Scotland a recent survey by Dight (1976) found that whereas 80 per cent of adult males had taken alcohol in the week prior to their interview, only 50 per cent of women had done likewise and the amounts reported consumed by women were between a third and a quarter of male intake.

As has been shown in Chapter One, although the reported quantities of alcohol drunk are unreliable underestimates, the overall classification of women as being more moderate and less frequent consumers of alcohol than men is indisputable. Indeed, examples of this difference can be found throughout the world, in both industrialized and 'primitive' societies. In a few tribal societies, such as the Abipone and Choroti tribes of South America, drinking in women is totally forbidden. In a number of others, such as the Bantu Tiriki tribe, women, being mere tribal appendages of a rank similar to that of witches and pre-pubertal boys, only take alcohol clandestinely; which for these women means surreptitiously swallowing the dregs of the beer produced by them for male beer drinking ceremonies (Sangree, 1962). Although in the majority of anthropological studies the sex differences in drinking habits are not as marked, they do exist, and the important question to consider is why this universal pattern should have occurred.

Bacon (1976) in a comprehensive review of alcohol use in tribal societies concluded that a number of factors were associated with the difference in male and female drinking dispositions, of which the almost universal concern of women with child care was found to be the major restriction on female drinking. This aspect has been well expressed by Child, Barry, and Bacon (1965: 60), who noted in their anthropological investigation of sex differences in the drinking habits of tribal societies that:

'it seems reasonable to expect that most societies would limit drinking and drunkenness in women more than in men. Under the generally prevailing conditions of human life, temporary incapacity of women is more threatening than is temporary incapacity of men. For example care of a field may be postponed for a day but care of a child cannot. The general social role of the sexes makes drunkenness more threatening in women than in men.'

This feature of female drinking has been further developed by Knupfer (1964) who made the important distinction that although the first part of the prescribed female role – that of homemaker – may only be moderately impaired by heavy alcohol consumption there is no doubt that excessive drinking of alcohol grossly interrupts the sensitivity to the needs of others, that is, the essential feature of the second part of the female role – that of child rearer.

There is also a further source of bias against women taking alcohol, in that drinking in women is often viewed as being associated with promiscuity, or at least a lessening of sexual restraint. This attitude was emphatically stated by William Cobbett who, in his advice to young men, wrote in the eighteenth century about women that: 'one who tips off the liquour with an appetite and exclaims good, good, by a smack of her lips, is fit for nothing but a brothal.'

It is necessary to note that this association between drinking and sexual freedom in women is more alluded to than investigated, and Gomberg (1976a) appropriately noted that women who are sexually available may have to socialize in drinking situations in order to make appropriate male contacts.

There are, therefore, in terms of drinking behaviour, a number of restraints operating against women, and it is possible to argue that the roles commonly adopted by men and women in the familial divisions of labour are centrally implicated in the very evident differences in drinking disposition. Consequently any change in roles will result in alteration of male and female drinking habits. As is well documented in Chapter One, such change is currently occurring and although it can be shown that since the 1950s there has been a marked increase in the frequency and amount that women drink, it still remains to be demonstrated that this change in behaviour has resulted in any marked 'softening' of attitudes about female drinking, especially that of a heavy nature. Dight (1976) in her Scottish Drinking Habit survey showed that both drinking and drunkenness were viewed less favourably in women than in men. With regard to drunkenness, 90 per cent of males and 93 per cent of females agreed with the statement that a drunken woman was a far more disgusting sight than a drunken man. Furthermore, a surprising 49 per cent of women – but only 39 per cent of men – believed that it was degrading for a woman to be seen drinking in a public house. This latter finding is no doubt an extreme one which would not be held so strongly south of the border; yet Cartwright, Shaw, and Spratley (1975) produced similar findings about drunkenness in their South London study, so it would appear that lowered tolerance of female drunkenness is a national trait. It is worthwhile noting that women tend to be more critical of women drinking excessively than are men, and this has obvious implications for women with drink problems.

It is relevant to record that these more conservative attitudes to women drinking are very pervasive and can be demonstrated to exist in even young children. For example, Jahoda and Crammond (1972) in their investigation of school children's knowledge of alcohol found that from a very early age parents encouraged their sons, but not their daughters, to use alcohol and as a consequence girls generally 'lag' behind boys in terms of their drinking experience. Davies and Stacey (1972) in their survey study of teenagers' attitudes and drinking habits, found that although most adolescents remembered their first experience of alcohol as occurring between the ages of thirteen and fourteen years, 47 per cent of boys but only 27 per cent of girls reported first tasting alcohol before this modal age. Moreover, Davies and Stacey (1972) found in their preliminary group discussion with their sample, that the teenagers considered heavy drinking and drunkenness more appropriate in men than in women.

In their full-scale investigation, in which the attitudes of approximately 1,400 teenagers were assessed, Davies and Stacey (1972) found that teenage girls were generally more accepting of heavy drinking in males than were boys, and that heavy drinking was perceived by most respondents as a masculine behaviour since it was seen as being 'tough' and 'rebellious' – traits which were considered by both sexes as more desirable in boys than girls. In addition sexes tended to accept what Davies and Stacey termed the 'alcohol myth' factor – 'its only natural for a man to like beer'; 'there's something manly about boys who drink'. Similarly, O'Connor (1978) in her study of Irish and English young drinkers, found that both parental and peer pressures were at work to restrict alcohol taking in young females. The adult double standard concerning drinking was evident in the teenagers studied, with both male and female disapproving of all-female drinking groups; drinking was viewed as an integral part of a male but not a female life-style.

Although recent evidence (Hawker, 1978) shows that the actual drinking behaviour of male and female teenagers is not greatly different and Saunders and Kershaw (1978) found that females aged 15-17 years actually reported drinking more than their male counterparts, there is no doubt that there is less tolerance of female drinking, especially if this reaches heavy or excessive levels. Appreciation of these general attitudes to high alcohol consumption by women is considered as essential in the understanding of many of the psychological features that are associated with alcohol-related problems in women. Given the existence of well-entrenched societal, attitudinal, and individual constraints against women drinking heavily, the question then becomes, what prompts some women to indulge in drinking to such an extent that they become labelled as 'alcoholics'?

Alcoholism and women

Any attempt at considering this question from a psychological perspective is confounded by a number of issues. Perhaps the most important confounding variable is that definitions of alcoholism have changed and previously-held views about the nature of alcoholism have also undergone considerable reformulation. One such changing perspective of alcoholism is the belief that alcoholism is a discrete entity which can be diagnosed by reference to a number of hallmark symptoms. The recent World Health Organisation publication (Edwards *et al.*, 1977) emphasizes that the nature of alcohol problems vary from person to person, and that the type of disabilities experienced by the individual depend to a large extent on the social milieu of the individual. This current thinking avoids notions of a fixed symptomology, and although some core symptoms obviously do exist, they may not necessarily be exhibited by all alcoholics. Recognition of this flexibility of diagnosis makes any generalization about alcoholics more difficult, since it is possible that any previously reported significant differences between, for example groups of male and female alcoholics, may well have been a function of the criteria used to differentiate the groups, and were not 'real' findings.

Furthermore, not only are the conceptualizations of the nature of alcoholism changing but it is also possible that the people who are currently developing alcohol problems are different from those who developed such problems in the past. It is possible to argue that in situations where per capita alcohol intake is low, those people who do over-indulge to a sufficient degree to develop 'alcoholism' represent an abnormal population in that their excessive drinking is motivated by psychological or personality factors. Excessive alcohol taking is thus a secondary condition, and any investigation of diagnosed alcoholics could show pre-alcoholic traits such as psychoneuroses, personality disorder, or affective illness. This could be especially true for women, for given the stronger taboos against their drinking, it may be that in times of low per capita consumption considerable disturbance is necessary to push the individual into heavy drinking. However, in a period of rising per capita consumption, which is associated with changes in women's roles and increased female alcohol intake, it is possible that more psychiatrically normal women will, for a variety of reasons, become involved in heavy drinking.

Such reasons could include occupation, since Plant (1979) has shown that the nature of one's employment has considerable influence upon one's drinking disposition, with persons in the production and selling of alcohol being 'at risk' of developing alcohol problems. Other occupations, such as sales representatives and company directors, are also vulnerable, and given the increased employment opportunities for women it may well be that this factor will become of increasing influence in the future.

Furthermore it has also been argued by Skog (1973) that alcohol habits are transmitted from person to person, with any increase in consumption by one individual putting pressure on neighbours and friends also to increase their intake. Thus increased alcohol intake may be spread by neighbours unwittingly encouraging each other to take alcohol rather than other beverages.

Since per capita consumption has rapidly risen since 1950, and is projected to continue to rise by approximately five per cent per annum (Mesdag, 1979), and as female drinking becomes more widely 'the norm' and thus accepted, it is highly likely that the female 'alcoholic' of today and the future will be different from her counterpart of earlier, more abstemious decades. In fact in any reading of the literature concerning the psychology, or psychopathology, of female alcoholics, one is struck by the idea that many investigators are attempting to clarify and refine an elusive and changing phenomenon. For example, Karpman, writing in 1948, was convinced that those women who developed alcoholism at that time were considerably more disturbed and psychiatrically abnormal than were male alcoholics. Yet the more recent literature (e.g. Wanberg and Horn, 1970; Gomberg, 1976b), produces little compelling evidence to suggest that women alcoholics exhibit markedly different psychopathology from their male counterparts. This is not to say that differences do not exist for, as will be illustrated, psychological factors do vary between male and female problem drinkers, but those differences that do exist may well reflect social influences in the development and presentation of alcoholism in women, rather than a prior greater psychopathology.

Psychology and women

For many reasons a single model or theory that encapsulated 'the psychology of women' would be most desirable. Unfortunately no such acceptable model exists, since the most pervasive and influential theory – that of the Freudian School – has been, of late, most vigorously criticized. There can be no doubt that Freud, and his adherents, emphatically supported the concept of male superiority. This bias was so great that, even allowing for the advantage of hindsight, it is difficult to comprehend how such theorizing could be so widely accepted and enthusiastically promulgated.

For example, Freud described the normal *healthy* female personality as being narcissistic, dependent, masochistic, and characterized by inhibited hostility and low self-esteem. Such traits were considered as stemming from the crisis of discovering the anatomical difference between the sexes, and the realization by women that they lack a penis. The Freudian zeitgeist can be judged by Millet's comment that 'His entire psychology of women, from which all modern psychology and psychoanalysis derives heavily, is built upon an original tragic experience – born female' (1972: 80).

She supports this statement by quoting from the collected papers of Freud (Riviere, 1959: 323): 'Women regard themselves as wronged from infancy, as underservably cut short and set back, and embitterment of so many daughters against their mothers derives in the last analysis from the reproach against her of having brought them into the world as women instead of men.'

Given such thinking it is not to be wondered that some feminist writers have totally rejected psychology as being of any value whatsoever in the understanding of women. Weisstein (1977: 206) notes, 'Psychologists have set about describing the true nature of women with a certainty and a sense of their own infallibility rarely found in the secular world'.

She illustrates her argument by citing a number of respected sources including Erikson (1964), whose views on female fulfilment rest totally on the biological function of women to produce and raise the children of men. This argument was also the basis of Rheingold's attack on the women's movement, when he noted (1968: 714):

'Anatomy decrees the life of a woman ... when women grow up without dread of their biological functions and without subversion by feminist doctrine, and therefore enter upon motherhood with a sense of fulfilment and altruistic sentiment we shall attain the goal of a good life and a secure world in which to live it.'

Such a statement, however ludicrous, is in complete accord with Freudian theory, in that women's roles in our society are seen as being biologically determined – anatomy as destiny. What is surprising about Rheingold's quotation is that it was seriously formulated some fifty years after Freud first espoused his own views on women. At least one can defend Freud's view by noting that evidence available at the time clearly showed marked differences in male and female achievement and attainment. For example, Ellis (1904) in an investigation of British genius could name only fifty-five women out of his total group of 1,030 geniuses, and a study undertaken in the same decade of the 1,000 most eminent people in the world included only thirty-two women. Furthermore, a report of 870 historically-famous women (Castle, 1913), showed that the vast majority of these women obtained their eminent status through birthright, or being the wives, mothers, or mistresses of famous men.

Such data reflecting the lack of female achievement could well encourage a view that women are both physically and psychologically inferior, and that this inferiority could stem from biological differences. However, since the 1920s there has been a steady accumulation of reliable, scientifically-obtained evidence which clearly demonstrates that on the majority of investigated variables there are no marked psychological differences between the sexes. For example Maccoby and Jacklin (1974), in their comprehensive review of the psychology of sex differences, found that in terms of intellectual processes such as perception, learning and memory, or other psychological factors such as sociability, self-esteem, achievement motivation, fear, timidity, compliance, or competitiveness the overall conclusion was one of 'no difference'. This is not to suggest that some differences do not seem to be reliably determined. For example, boys are usually found to be more physically and verbally aggressive, and girls tend to do better on tests of verbal ability; but from a psychological perspective the sexes are more alike than they are dissimilar, and certainly the marked differences in sex roles and attainment appear to be due to other factors. Weisstein (1977: 214) succinctly notes: 'In brief the uselessness of present psychology with regard to women is simply a special case of the general conclusion: one must understand social expectation about women if one is going to characterize the behaviour of women.'

Weisstein's conclusion is of major relevance in any consideration of alcohol problems and women, since it is against a background of women's roles and social expectations that the nature of alcohol-related problems in women must be viewed. Changes in roles have altered female drinking habits and the nature of problems. As will be argued in the later parts of this chapter the general life-style of women is inextricably bound up with the prevalence of the so called 'mental illnesses' in women.

Psychological factors and alcoholism in women

With the provision concerning a probable change over time in the nature of female alcoholics well in mind, it is possible to examine some of the psychological factors commonly argued as being associated with alcoholism in women.

Familial incidence

One of the frequently occurring items in the literature is the finding that female alcoholics are raised in families where a parent or sibling is also alcoholic. Schuckit (1972), in a review of twenty-eight studies reporting data about female alcoholics, showed an increased rate of alcoholism in the first degree relatives of women alcoholics, with such rates being, in some reports, as high as 50 per cent in the fathers and brothers of the patients studied. Taken against a general expectancy rate of alcoholism in males of about 3-5 per cent these results are obviously significant. It has been recognized for some time that the drinking habits of parents are influential in determining the subsequent drinking behaviour of their children, and it would appear that both sexes may be adversely influenced, but interestingly the incidence of alcoholism appears to be higher in the family histories of female rather than male alcoholics. Cotton (1979), in a comprehensive review of the literature, found that seven out of nine studies which included comparative sex data showed a considerably higher rate of alcohol problems in the families of female alcoholics. In fact the two studies that failed to support this trend both reported unusually high rates (70 per cent) of male alcoholics with excessive drinking relatives.

Furthermore, there appears to be a greater incidence of general psychiatric illness and early childhood disruption in the families of female alcoholics than in those of male problem drinkers. For example, Winokur and Clayton (1967), in a comparative study of sixty-nine male and forty-five female alcoholics, reported that the female group were significantly more likely to have unknown, or psychiatrically ill parents, than were the male group. In addition, in the female group, increased rates of sociopathic personality in the male relatives, and depressive illnesses in female relatives were also found. The overall implication is that, in comparison to male alcoholics, women alcoholics can be shown to have more disturbed family backgrounds, with relatives exhibiting higher rates of alcoholism or psychiatric illness, and also increased rates of early parental loss. However, disturbed early childhood patterns are true of many psychiatric conditions and why some women develop alcoholism, and others different psychopathologies, still requires explanation.

Gender identity conflict

One such frequently occurring explanation is the concept that women alcoholics have difficulty in adjusting to their sexual identity, and that this difficulty is of etiological importance. Throughout the literature one is confronted with terms such as 'role confusion', 'incongruent femininity', 'feminine role rejection', 'over-identification with the feminine role', and 'masculine identification'. As may be appreciated, terminology abounds but clarity does not. It should be noted that researchers in this area have aided and abetted this lack of clarity by their inconsistent use of terminology, with the greatest confusion coming from the use of the term 'sex role'. For the purposes of this chapter, 'sex role' is used as reference to prescribed patterns of behaviour assigned to particular categories of individuals in a society. Thus child care is, in most societies, a 'sex role' of women. However, in many publications 'sex role' is incorrectly used as reference to gender identity, i.e. how the individual perceives his or her own sexual identity. In relation to alcohol problems it is this latter issue of sexual identity which has been regularly invoked as being of etiological importance. In an attempt to understand more fully this area it is necessary to consider a number of recent investigations. One such study was conducted by Wilsnack (1973) who tested twenty-eight alcoholic women and their matched controls on a variety of tests and concluded that alcoholic women overvalued the feminine role – a finding considered by the investigator as being consistent with earlier reports that women alcoholics are unconsciously more masculine than their alcohol problem-free peers. It was argued by Wilsnack (1973) that drinking is a response to this internal conflict, since it had been shown by the same author in an earlier study that, for women, drinking produced greater feminine imagery and decreased masculine assertiveness. This change toward more feminine type behaviour was assessed by responses on a projective test (the Thematic Apperception test). Without being unduly harsh about such techniques, it may be noted that such tests lack reliability, validity, and any indication of scientific rigour. It is thus possible seriously to question any hypothesis developed, or results obtained, from projective test usage.

Another study in this area is that of Parker (1972), who in an investigation of 102 matched female alcoholics and social drinkers, found on a masculinity and femininity test, that the alcoholic group had increased conscious masculine identity characteristics and reduced unconscious femininity. As may be appreciated this result is in the opposite direction to that of Wilsnack's (1973) reported above, but the inconsistency between these studies has been used by Sciada and Vannicelli (1978) to argue that the existence of this gender conflict, irrespective of direction, is the important factor in understanding female alcoholism. In their study, conflict, as measured by an inventory comprising of sexual identity adjectives and a projective test, was found to be associated with problem drinking, with the greater the conflict the greatest the tendency toward problem drinking. Unfortunately, association is used by the authors to argue cause and effect, in that conflict is seen as a determinant of heavy drinking. It is always wise to remember that association and cause are not the same thing, as can be demonstrated by the reported statistical fact that those areas of northern Europe with the highest birth rates also have the highest number of storks' nests. To argue that the latter is involved in the former is a romantic fallacy, with the more mundane explanation being that where dense population exists, the availability of suitable nesting sites in chimneys, and other building structures, also increases!

The work on gender identity and alcoholism may also be criticized on the grounds that the methods employed to ascertain 'femininity' and 'masculinity' are based on the assumption that such traits are bipolar, i.e. any individual may be placed on a dimension with extreme masculinity at one end and extreme femininity at the other. However it would appear that yet again the alcohology field has failed to keep abreast of developments in general behavioural science, since there is now a good case, succintly reviewed by Worrell (1978), to suggest that masculinity and femininity are independent, orthogonal dimensions. That is, any individual possesses both masculine and feminine characteristics, and that these can be measured as existing in varying amounts in the same individual. Overall masculinity/femininity traits may therefore be assessed as the extent to which one chooses a higher degree of one type of characteristic in preference to the other.

Failure to incorporate these recent developments into alcoholism research is an obvious error but there is also the telling criticism that, in the sexual identity conflict research available to date, it is very possible that consequence is being confused with cause. If one considers the disruption that ensues in the families of women with alcohol problems, it is not surprising that female alcoholics, when interviewed in alcoholism treatment agencies, display ambivalence about their sexual identity. Those norms internalized by all of us about women's roles in child rearing, are opposite to the central effect upon the family of female heavy drinking. Furthermore, attitudes about women drinking heavily, and the toll that excessive drinking may take in terms of sexual response or behaviour, may well induce confusion about an individual's sexual identity. 'Over-identification' with any sexual category may well be a result of the guilt and low self-esteem that are frequently recounted by women in such situations, and need not be reflective of a pre-disposing etiological factor.

What is required to gauge the importance of gender identity conflict as a cause of female alcoholism is a longitudinal study using reliable and valid measures of sexual identity. To date only one such longitudinal study, a report of the characteristics of teenagers who subsequently developed alcohol problems, has been reported. Jones (1971) analysed data obtained in the Oakland Growth Study and this investigation has often been cited as giving support to the concept that female problem drinkers over-identify with being feminine as teenagers, and that this eventually leads to frustration and drinking in later life. In fact any results from the Oakland Growth Study must be cautiously evaluated since the measurement of psychological traits of the sample were based on projective techniques and clinical assessment. Further criticism is that in this study the actual number of problem drinkers in the sample was only three. In addition the idea that future female problem drinkers could be detected by their 'ultrafemininity' as teenagers, came from the blind clinical assessment by one psychologist of data from a projective test of only one of the three subjects who later developed alcoholism. Therefore to state that their study is confirmation of the concept that alcoholic women exhibit over-positive attitudes towards the female role, toward femininity, and motherhood is to take anecdotalism to extreme, and the conclusion to date about gender conflict theorizing must be that the hypothesis is 'not proven'. Indeed, work in this area makes one recall Keller's Law, (1972: 1147) which alcoholism's acknowledged dean of words, summarized as follows:

'A splurge of reports in the 1940s, of biochemical character-istics purporting to differentiate alcoholics from non-alco-holics stimulated me to review a voluminous related litera-ture, implicating physical, social and psychological demarcators as well. The only conclusion I could derive, from the entirety of the reportage, took a form that became known, among colleagues, as Keller's Law: "The investigation of any trait in alcoholics will show that they have either more or less of it." Accordingly I then predicted that if sexadactyly should be investigated, alcoholics will yield either more or fewer six-toed and six-fingered people than a control group.'

This quotation is important since it reflects a consistent and developing trend in the alcoholism research field, which is the movement away from any attempt at searching for the 'alcoholic personality' or any predisposing factor that will single-handedly explain alcoholism

Part of this movement stems from a growing realization that alcoholism involves not only the drinker and the drug but also the environment in which it is consumed, and thus social factors may be of considerable importance in the presentation, duration, and treatment of alcohol problems. In addition, research of the above type makes the assumption that alcoholic women are an homogeneous group, and therefore their condition can, at least in the overwhelming majority of cases, be accounted for by a single theoretical position. As our understanding of the nature of alcoholism has become more complex, so such mono-causal explanations have lost attractiveness. There is, in fact, well documented evidence which clearly suggests that alcoholic women are not an homogeneous group and that alcoholism in women is variously caused and manifested. The most accepted practice is to describe two principal groups of alcoholic women, those of primary and secondary type, of which the latter are characterized by affective disorders which can in a high proportion of cases, be shown to pre-date the onset of alcoholismic drinking. Sclare (1970) in a retrospective study of fifty hospitalized female alcoholics, considered that 20 per cent of his sample could be demonstrated to have a pre-existing depressive illness, and a similar figure, 27 per cent, was reported by Schuckit, Pitts, and Reich (1969) in a study of seventy American in-patient female alcoholics. This group could be distinguished from primary alcoholics by their shorter duration of problems, younger age, and greater number of suicide attempts. In a further twelve cases, antedating psychiatric illness was evident, and thus less than 50 per cent of Schuckit *et al.*'s (1969) sample were diagnosed as being primary alcoholics. Such findings clearly question the validity of conceiving female alcoholics as a single unitary group, whose condition may be explained by a single cause. Such heterogeneity of group membership clearly suggests that a flexible and multifaceted theory of the etiology of alcoholism in women is necessary. Over the past decade the idea that the prevalence of alcohol problems may be related to per capita consumption has gained considerable support, and individual changes in alcohol consumption may be accounted for by a variety of social factors including type of employment, financial status, ethnic and parental background, social role, and the availability and cost of alcohol. Such socio-cultural theorizing about the nature of alcoholism is, because of its very flexibility and complexity, intuitively more satisfying than single state theories.

Social influences

Indeed, the invoking of a social, or socio-cultural perspective in the understanding of alcoholism in women provides a number of comparatively straightforward explanations for some of the characteristics that are frequently recorded as 'hallmarks' of female alcoholism. Although many of the common stereotypes of alcoholics, or beliefs about alcoholism, have been exposed as manifestly false, the common ideas about female alcoholics generally run true to form. For example, the idea that women are generally secret drinkers, imbibing their alcohol alone, at home, and during the day does appear, from clinical reports, to be correct. Wanberg and Horn (1970), in a comparative study of over 2,000 male and female problem drinkers, noted that their female patients consistently reported drinking as a solitary behaviour, undertaken at home. Such drinking is often interpreted as being more pathological than male excessive drinking, which at least has the facade of being social drinking, and there is a tendency, especially amongst patients, to look for reasons to explain or excuse such 'deviant' behaviour. In reality however, the very taboos that exist about women drinking at all, encourage heavy female consumers to drink in such a manner. Unable to visit the public house in the same casual way as her heavy drinking male counterpart the female problem drinker is 'forced' to drink at home, and the lack of suitable or available drinking companions often results in such drinking being a solitary affair. This well-known and accepted stereotype of female alcoholism is an additional burden for the female problem drinker who is then encouraged to deny, to herself and her significant others, the extent of her drinking behaviour. Fear of exposure to this prevailing stigma of female alcoholism no doubt also encourages attempts at secrecy, exhibited by the hiding of both the supply and the empty containers. This need for secrecy also precipitates different beverage use, such as gin or vodka, in an attempt to further avoid detection. The zeitgeist against women drinking heavily then causes additional troubles for females since having been 'forced' by social mores into greater secretive alcohol usage, therapists can be shown to be highly critical of women alcoholics since they are condemned as being less truthful about their alcohol intake, and prone to greater denial of their problems than are their male counterparts.

In some ways, however, the social taboo against female drinking may benefit women alcoholics, since many studies of female excessive drinkers indicate that, in comparison to males, this group have telescoped drinking histories, i.e. women appear to develop alcoholism symptoms more rapidly.

The evidence is that women generally report their onset of symptoms as occurring later in life, though they are often, at presentation or first psychiatric contact, of a similar age – approximately forty-forty-five years – as male alcoholics. This difference in the duration of problems can be argued as being indicative of favourable prognosis since it has been demonstrated by Costello (1975) that patients reporting shorter drinking histories also exhibit less social and psychological damage and subsequently fare better in treatment. However the comparatively shorter duration of problems in women alcoholics may be variously explained. Some authors, for example Lindbeck (1972) and Beckman (1975), have argued that the evidence from clinical studies of female alcoholics suggests that the shorter drinking histories of women are indicative of an accelerated progression through the stages of alcoholism and that on presentation at hospitals or alcohol treatment agencies, female alcoholics exhibit as severe symptoms of their condition as do men, and this quicker attainment of chronic signs is suggestive of greater initial psychopathology. Alternatively, this more rapid attainment of chronic signs could be due to physiological differences between men and women, and as shown in chapter two, there is evidence that women are physically more susceptible to the adverse effects of alcohol.

However, a case can also be made for the hypothesis that the earlier presentation, in terms of duration of problems, for women is a function of the complex process of hospital or agency referral, in which severity of illness is just one factor, and perhaps a minor one in relation to social influences. It may well be the case that the immediate social milieu of the majority of women alcoholics is considerably more concerned about female excessive drinking, because the social role of women makes such drinking more noticeable. Furthermore, whereas male heavy drinking may often be considered as 'normal', the equivalent behaviour in females is less tolerantly viewed as 'madness', and hence requires quick and active intervention. There is some evidence from epidemiological studies to support the contention that women are more likely than men to seek, or be encouraged to seek, psychiatric help.

For example, Edwards, Chandler and Hensman (1972) in their community survey of drinking habits and problems in Camberwell detected a male to female ratio of alcoholism of eight males to every one female alcoholic, but much lower (usually 4:1) ratios for hospital admissions are commonly reported. Similarly, a recent Scottish investigation has recorded male to female ratios of 9:1 in the community, 5:1 in terms of hospital referral, and 3:1 with regard to hospital admissions. Although differences between male to female ratios in community and hospital studies could be due to failure to detect female alcoholics in the community, it is also possible that these figures may reflect real differences in the use of services. The difference in referral ratios and hospital admission ratios noted above could also be indicative of greater concern about female drinking by both public and the medical practitioners concerned, which is reflected in the greater willingness of hospital doctors to admit female alcoholics for treatment.

That social factors play a role in the presentation of psychiatric conditions can be seen from investigations of other psychiatric illnesses. For example, the peak of admissions for schizophrenic illnesses is at an earlier age for males than it is for psychotic women. It is superficially tempting to believe that this is a reflection of an earlier manifestation of symptoms in males than in females, but a study by Raskin and Golob (1966) indicated that although males were admitted at a younger age than females, detailed investigation of the history of the patients' illnesses showed that females evinced symptoms of schizophrenia at a similar age to that of the male sample. The difference in actual age of referral was considered by Raskin and Golob to be due to the fact that the social roles of teenage boys – primarily being concerned with establishing themselves in employment – made any withdrawal due to psychotism more conspicuous, whereas any social timidity in females was seen as being due to shyness or late social development.

There are, of course, other social factors involved in the admission process for women drinkers. The spouses of female excessive drinkers are far more able, through both vested authority and physical strength, to insist on their wives' attendance at the general practitioners or an alcohol treatment agency. Moreover, very disparate legal, economic, and social factors often inhibit wives of drinking spouses taking similar positive action. In the event, understanding of this telescoped symptom presentation in women may need to take account of both explanations, with some female alcoholics having accelerated alcohol careers because of greater psychopathology or physiological susceptibility, and others being comparatively quickly 'motivated' into treatment because of social factors. Once again, viewing women alcoholics as a heterogeneous group may provide parsimonious explanations for apparently conflicting viewpoints.

Further comment is also necessary on the apparent late onset of symptoms in female alcoholics. Survey investigations of alcoholism in the community show that the majority of male problem drinkers are aged under twenty-five (e.g. see Cahalan and Room, 1974) but in females their drinking and problems often increased later on in life, especially in the early thirties and forties as Cahalan (1970: 42) notes:

'These differences between men and women are consistent with the inference that while men may generally get introduced to heavier drinking by other men when they are young, women more often get involved in heavier drinking relatively later, perhaps as a result of their husbands' or men friends' influence.'

Indeed support for this latter idea can be culled from the recent 'Rand Report' (Armor, Polich, and Stambul, 1978) which showed that the most striking differences in terms of client characteristics between men and women was that whereas 17 per cent of male alcoholics, and 32 per cent of male problem drinkers, reported that their spouses were heavy drinkers, for female alcoholics 35 per cent reported their spouses as being heavy alcohol users, and 63 per cent of female problem drinkers reported likewise. Such disparate social characteristics are hard to ignore and clearly suggest that spouses' drinking has a stronger precipitating role in female rather than male alcoholism.

A further important psychological factor in the presentation and management of alcoholism in women is the existence of inimical levels of low self-esteem. A number of research investigations and clinical reports have consistently highlighted low self-concept as being considerably more evident in female as compared to male alcoholics. Indeed low self-esteem has been highlighted as a factor which is considered to pre-date the onset of a number of psychiatric illnesses in women, and it has been suggested as being a chronic condition for women in general (e.g. Bardwick, 1971).

As far as alcoholism is concerned, it is possible to consider low self-esteem as either a cause or a consequence of excessive drinking. As a sequela of heavy drinking, low self-esteem in women is not difficult to understand. The existing taboos and increased stigmas against female heavy drinking, coupled with the greater disruption of family life and the often marked and very evident deterioration in the physical appearance of female alcoholic patients, results in many patients exhibiting very high levels of anxiety, guilt, self-reproachment, and despair. Beck's (1974) triad of depressive symptomatology – self seeming worthless, outer world meaningless, and the future hopeless – are sadly all too often very evidently present in female alcoholics, and this is reflected in the higher incidence of self-poisoning attempts in women. Clinical experience shows that many women in the early stages of their treatment are often bewildered by their own recent behaviour and spend considerable time in attempts at rationalizing or justifying such behaviour. This confusion is generally not aided by the inclusion of such patients in groups of alcoholics largely composed of males with distinctly different drinking habits, social problems, and psychological needs. Such practice tends only to further convince the female alcoholic of her own 'oddness' and lack of worth.

Self-esteem and women

The problem of self-esteem in women alcoholics warrants further comment since it is possible that such negative self-images stem from both the greater stigmatization of women excessive drinkers and also from the very nature of self-esteem. Although it has been proposed that the roles of women in society prevent them from achieving self-satisfying roles in life, research in this area generally fails to endorse the hypothesis that women have lower self-images than men. For example Kaplan (1973) in a study of 500 adults living in Texas could find no overall difference between men and women respondents on a self-derogation-low-esteem scale. Although some sex differences were evident these were associated with factors such as education and race, and this finding appears to be consistently reported in the literature.

Maccoby and Jacklin (1974) analysed thirty studies concerned with self-esteem which were undertaken between 1961-1973 and concluded that males and females have equally positive (or negative) self-images and that there was no good evidence for Bardwick's (1971) assertion that women have lower self-esteem than men. Given that such a difference remains to be conclusively demonstrated, there is some evidence which suggests that the basis or source of self-esteem may well vary between the sexes. Thus Carlson (1970) in an investigation of self-esteem, used an adjective check list to determine those qualities that subjects thought were descriptive of themselves. The adjectives used were considered by Carlson (1970) to assess either social or personal sources of self-evaluation. Adjectives of a personal type were those such as 'independent, practical, ambitious, confident, imaginative and fairminded', whereas those of a social nature were adjectives such as 'co-operative, friendly, tactful, sympathetic and dependable'. As may be seen, social adjectives infer social interaction, whereas the personal adjectives are primarily concerned with self rather than others. In a series of investigations Carlson (1970) discovered that women, irrespective of age, generally described themselves in terms of social, or interpersonal adjectives, whereas the male subjects responded in terms of self or individualistic adjectives. Carlson therefore concluded that although the level of self-esteem may be assessed as being the same between the sexes, the sources of their self-evaluation were very different.

As an act of conjecture, it is possible to suggest that the very evident clinical differences in self-esteem between male and female alcoholics could be due to a combination of the prevailing stigma about heavy drinking in women being exacerbated by the fact that the excessive drinking grossly impairs the sources of self-esteem for women. Thus women who rely on feedback from their significant others as a measure of their self-worth, receive negative images since their drinking has an immediate and inimical effect upon such relationships. The male alcoholic, who draws his self-evaluation from a more individual perspective may well receive better 'messages', since he can still convince himself about being tough, 'one of the boys', or masculine, and his self-image is correspondingly less disrupted. Indeed, it is possible to conceive that even a prolonged history of heavy drinking may leave the male self-image relatively intact.

Locus of control and women

Although it has been argued that self-images cannot be demonstrated as being different between men and women prior to the onset of alcoholism, there are a number of associated psychological variables that are consistently demonstrated as being different for the sexes. Given equality of self esteem, it might be assumed that men and women would have equal levels of confidence about their abilities to cope when confronted with various psychological tasks. However Maccoby and Jacklin (1974) convincingly show that on tests of confidence in task performance men generally exhibit greater levels of confidence in their ability to succeed. For example, male university students when assessed on tests of geometric problem-solving or anagram solution are consistently more likely to report that they expect to do well, even if the test is one on which males generally perform worse than women. This lack of confidence in their performance level can also be demonstrated by asking women how they expect to fare in university examinations. Although the examination results clearly indicate that in general women are better students than men, when asked about potential exam performance the former are found to be more pessimistic than their fellow male students. Although various explanations may be advanced for this apparent discrepancy, (for instance that men are more boastful, or that they value academic success more) there is a developing belief that the apparent paradox between equal levels of self-esteem but inferior (and unjustified) self-confidence levels in women may be explained in terms of the extent to which people feel they control, or are responsible for, their own lives. Measurement of the feelings people have about how much they control their own destinies has shown that two categories of people exist. Some people feel they are in control of their fate, and thus any achievements they may attain are the result of their own efforts; whereas a second group can be distinguished who feel that their lives are outwith their control, and that any events that occur are a result of chance or good or bad luck. This type of research – generally known as 'locus of control' (Rohsenow and O'Leary, 1978) – shows that adult women tend to be 'externalizers', i.e. their successes are seen as being due to 'good fortune' and are not reflections of their own skills; whereas adult men are generally 'internalizers', i.e. feel that they are in control of their own destinies and that any derived attainment is a just reward for their efforts. Jacklin and Mischel (1973) argue that this apparent greater belief by men in their ability to control their own destiny is part of our cultural stereotype of maleness. As evidence they report an investigation of stories in school textbooks, which showed that good events in the lives of male characters were directly linked to the characters' own actions, whereas girls were seen as having good things happen to them because of the actions of others, or as an indirect consequence of passing events. Interestingly, locus of control theorizing has recently been incorporated into models of mental illness.

The most influential of these theories is that of 'learned help-lessness', which has been applied to a number of conditions, but especially that of depression. Simply stated, the 'learned help-lessness' hypothesis as formulated by Seligman (1975), suggests that if individuals are placed in situations where their actions have no influence on the course of events, then as they become aware of this they tend to abandon any attempts at mastering their situation. This lapse into helplessness is also accompanied with increased levels of depression and anxiety, since the indivi-dual is uncertain as to what will occur in the future.

Evidence in support of this theory was initially drawn from animal work, and marked performance and emotional deficits were evident when animals were subjected to non-contingent (i.e. the responses to the animals were not linked to the animals' behaviour) reinforcement schedules. Work with human subjects (e.g. Gatchel and Proctor, 1976, and Miller and Seligman, 1976) has tended to support the concept of 'learned helplessness' but in many cases the results are not as marked as those from animal studies. The typical experimental paradigm used with human subjects is for subjects to receive a training phase which is followed by a test phase. In the training phase subjects are exposed to either:

(i) contingent reinforcement – i.e. events in the subjects' environment are a consequence of the subjects' behaviour; or

(ii) non-contingent reinforcement – i.e. the subjects' perfor-mance does not influence events.

On conclusion of this training phase, subjects are tested on various tasks – such as anagram solutions or copying designs with blocks – and the performance of the different groups is then compared. 'Learned helplessness' is deemed to exist when the performance of the non-contingent group of subjects, when assessed against the performance of the subjects in the contin-gent group, is impaired. Thus 'learned helplessness' refers to the performance deficits caused by exposure to non-contingent out-comes.

Miller and Norman (1979) reviewed twenty-three studies of the above type and concluded, with reservations, that the data from human subjects supported the 'learned helplessness' model in that the majority of studies did show the occurrence of behavioural deficits in the predicted direction. A further six studies also found emotional factors to be more prevalent in the non-contingently reinforced groups, but although depression and anxiety were evident, so were increased levels of hostility, which had not previously been predicted by Seligman's theory.

However a more telling criticism of Seligman's formulation of 'learned helplessness' was that it failed to take cognisance of the individual's attribution of the reasons for his/her failure, and emphasized the situational effect of non-contingent response as being the crucial variable in the determination of 'learned helplessness'. Levis (1976) has succinctly pointed out that this may be true for animals, but to extrapolate to human subjects is to equate the cognitive processes of humans with those of a cockroach. Thus the individual in a 'learned helplessness' experimental paradigm has the ability to determine, rightly or wrongly the cause of his/her predicament. A person may well realize that their responses are not influential in determining outcome and can therefore blame themselves (I keep getting it wrong) or outside interference (the experimenter is controlling the situation). Not surprisingly, it has been shown that the latter appreciation of the situation is less harmful in terms of one's view of oneself than is the former, and also less likely to result in 'learned helplessness' occurring. Seligman has, in the light of this criticism, modified his formulation of 'learned helplessness' (Abramson, Seligman and Teasdale, 1978) and it is relevant to consider the effect of this reformulation in terms of its implications for women.

It can be demonstrated that there is a sex difference in the use of explanations for failure outcomes in non-contingent reinforcement. Dweck and Repucci (1973) and Dweck and Bush (1976) found that boys tended to attribute their failure to effort, whereas girls considered it was their ability which was at fault. Weiner, Nierenberg, and Goldstein (1976) have shown that the attribution of causality to non-stable items – such as effort which is considered to vary over time, as compared to stable items, e.g. ability or intelligence, which is perceived as fixed – results in less affective disturbance. As noted previously, it would appear that in situations of 'good outcome' males tend to use stable explanations of causality such as due to ability, whereas females see such events being due to 'chance', or 'good fortune', which are unstable attributions, and thus the outcome is not positively incorporated into one's perception of oneself. This argument is summarized by Miller and Norman (1979: 109-110) as follows:

> 'If one attributes past outcomes to luck (a variable cause) then these outcomes will not influence one's expectancies in future situations, but if one attributes past outcomes to ability (a stable outcome) then one's expectancies for performance in future situations will shift in the direction of outcome. [Experimental] results suggest that stability of attribution mediates the degree of influence that past outcomes exert on expectancies for performance in future situations.'

Simply explained it would appear that the evidence to date suggests that males use variable causes to explain failure outcomes, and stable causes to account for good outcomes. For women the reverse seems true. The implication of this is that women are caught both ways – they play down good events in their lives as being due to external forces and take to heart failure outcomes which they perceive as stemming from their own weaknesses. If this hypothesis is true, and the experimental evidence to date is only suggestive, it would go some way toward explaining the higher rates in women of some psychiatric illnesses, of which depression is a commonly quoted example since it is generally two to three times more prevalent in women than in men.

'Mental illnesses' and women

The importance of this for our understanding of alcoholism is that it is highly probable that as the difference between the roles of men and women continues to decrease, there may well be a substitution of 'illnesses', with those 'illnesses' such as depression, which are currently open to women, being replaced by male 'illnesses' such as alcoholism. Thus explanations such as 'learned helplessness', may well become of significant importance in attempting to understand a rise in the rate of female alcoholism. Indeed it has already been noted by Weissman and Klerman (1977: 103) that:

> 'While depression is more common in women, alcohol use and abuse are considerably more common in men. It has been

hypothesized that depression and alcoholism are different but equivalent disorders . . . environmental factors may render it difficult for women to drink excessively. In families that discourage drinking by women, the same illness might manifest itself as depression rather than alcoholism.'

There have been over the past decade a number of attempts to apply 'locus of control' research to the alcoholism field. To date such research is very much in its infancy and it is necessary to note that many of the findings are inconclusive, with the suggestion being that when compared to control groups, alcoholics are 'externalizers', but they become more 'internal' over treatment (Rohsenow and O'Leary 1978). However, perhaps the important contribution of this type of research is that it has developed from the scientific study of 'normal' people and is currently being applied to 'abnormal' populations such as alcoholics. This is a considerable improvement when compared to the traditional psychiatric approach of theorizing about 'abnormal' clinical populations without any understanding of what constitutes normality.

Furthermore, this type of approach perceives psychological factors as co-existing with other important variables, especially those of a sociological nature. For example Jessor *et al.*, (1968) and subsequently Cahalan (1970) have attempted to incorporate psychological factors within broader sociological concepts such as deviancy. Based on the deviancy theory of Cloward and Ohlin (1960), Jessor *et al.* (1968), in their study of three different ethnic communities in Colorado, proposed that the prevalence of excessive drinking was associated with the obtainability of a society's prescribed goals. If the valued goals were readily accessible via approved means or channels, then deviant behaviour was likely to be infrequent, but if access was restricted or denied to part of a community, then there was an increased likelihood of deviant behaviour occurring, especially in those individuals who's sub-culture supported deviant behaviour and who possessed psychological traits such as impulsivity, or external 'locus of control'. This interplay of sociological and psychological factors has been further developed by Cahalan. In his reports of the drinking habits and problems of a national American sample (Cahalan, 1970; Cahalan and Room, 1974), six composite variables were utilized to explain variations of drinking disposition and alcohol-related problems. These six variables illustrate the interaction between individual and societal factors which can be appreciated from the names assigned to these variables; namely, attitudes towards drinking, environmental support for heavy drinking, alienaton and maladjustment, unfavourable expectations, looseness of social controls, and impulsiveness and non-conformity.

Cahalan (1970: 141-142) duly noted that:

> 'In general the findings bear out the conclusion that both sociological and psychological factors are important in the development of problem drinking. The sociological – that is to say the external, environmental – factors determine whether the individual is encouraged or permitted to drink heavily; and the psychological factors can operate to help bring about or maintain the level of drinking which may be above that normally encouraged or permitted for the person's environment.'

Having referred earlier to a possible substitution of illnesses, with alcohol problems replacing depression as a female illness, it is relevant to note that the research into the causes and maintenance of depression has become increasingly focused on interaction between psychological and social factors, and it may well be that these will, in time, be implicated in alcoholism. For example, concepts such as 'learned helplessness', which are based on the supposed longstanding effect of women's disadvantaged social status, can be supported by evidence from the differential rates of mental illness among married and unmarried women.

The argument is that if mental illness is related to the disadvantages inherent in women's roles then married women, who are more likely to typify the traditional stereotyped role, should exhibit higher rates of mental illness than married men or single women. In a series of reports Gove and his colleagues (Gove, 1972, 1973; and Gove and Tudor, 1973) examined American mental health statistics obtained from community surveys and hospital admission data. They found that the higher overall rates of many mental illnesses for females were largely accounted for by higher rates for married women. Gove and Tudor (1973: 66) in their review of sex roles and mental illness note:

'The information on first admissions to mental hospitals, psychiatric treatment in general hospitals, psychiatric out-patients' clinics, private outpatient psychiatric care, the prac-tices of general physicians, and community surveys all indi-cate that more women than men are mentally ill . . . However, all these studies indicate that married women were more likely to have a mental disorder than married men. The results were quite different for unmarried persons. When never married men were compared with never married women, divorced men with divorced women, and widowed men with widowed women it was found that within each of these statuses . . . that men were more likely than women to be mentally ill.'

The clear implication is that marriage has a protective effect for males but a detrimental effect for women. It is generally argued that the disadvantages of the married female role stem from several factors, of which Gove and Tudor (1973) consider role restriction, i.e. married women occupy one role, that of homemaker, whereas married men have both home and work roles, as the most important. This role restriction results in women being trapped in a low prestige 'occupation' – house-work, and child care – and even if the wife does work it is gener-ally in a non-career job which is less highly valued than her husband's employment.

Not only are married female roles restricted but it has been shown by Brown, Bhrolchain, and Harris (1975) and Brown and Harris (1978) that other domestic factors are also involved in the etiology of depression. Using data obtained from a community study they found that working-class married women who were looking after young children had the highest rates of depression. Examination of the effect of social class on depression showed that given equal levels of stress, working-class married women were five times more at risk of becoming depressed than were middle-class women. Four factors were found to account for this class difference, namely having three or four children under the age of fourteen living at home, loss of mother in childhood, lack of employment outside the home, and the absence of an intimate and confiding relationship with their spouse or boy-friend. Brown, *et al.* suggest that a close and emotionally supportive relationship with their men was of considerable prophylactic importance in preventing depression in women. In addition, working away from the home was also seen as giving an immunity to affective illness since it presented opportunities for women to increase their independence, social contacts, and self-esteem.

Conclusion

Evidence such as this implicates the social role of women in the etiology of mental 'illness', and it is considered that understanding alcoholism in women from a perspective in which psychological factors are seen as being associated with the social context of women, allows for a more complex understanding of any future 'explosion' in the prevalence of alcoholism in women. Unfortunately from this perspective it would appear that this explosion is almost inevitable. To borrow again from the literature concerning depression Weissman and Kerlman (1977: 108) note:

'Rising expectations, access to new opportunities, and efforts to redress the social irregularities of women have been suggested as further explanation for the recent increase in depression among women. Depressions may occur not when things are at their worst, but when there is a possibility of improvement, and a discrepancy between one's rising aspirations and the likelihood of fulfilling these wishes . . . new role expectations may also create intrapsychic personal conflicts, particularly for those women involved in traditional family tasks but who also desire employment and recognition outside the family.'

Furthermore, if as has been suggested, psychosocial models, such as 'learned helplessness', are of relevance in understanding alcohol problems in women, then it would be a considerable error to believe that simple and effective remedies are available to cause a reduction in such problems. Banning alcohol advertising or restricting supermarket sales will not alter inimical life-styles or relieve deep seated, culturally induced, frustrations. Within the alcoholism field and especially in regard to the minority areas, such as women and teenagers, there is an urgent need to move away from a 'what's wrong with them' and develop a wider perspective. Too many clinicians and counsellors adhere to the belief that human behaviour is determined by an individual and internal dynamic, rather than by an interplay between the individual and his or her social milieu. To understand, and then appropriately respond to women with alcohol problems requires an appreciation of the social context of women. How women behave will, in general, be a function of what people expect women to be, and how society values their contribution. As Weisstein (1977: 208) has noted: 'Compared to the influence of the social context within which a person lives, his or her history and traits, as well as biological make-up, may simply be random variations, noise superimposed on the true signal that can predict behaviour.'

References

Abramson, L., Seligman, M., and Teasdale, J. (1978) Learned Helplessness in Humans: Critique and Reformulation. *Journal of Abnormal Psychology* **87**: 49-74.

Armor, D., Polich, J., and Stambul, H. (1978) *Alcoholism and Treatment*. New York: Wiley Interscience.

Bacon, M. (1976) Alcohol Use in Tribal Societies. In B. Kissin and H. Begleiter, *The Biology of Alcoholism*. Vol. 4. New York: Plenum Press.

Bardwick, J. (1971) *Psychology of Women*. New York: Harper & Row.

Beckman, L. (1975) Women Alcoholics: A Review of Social and Psychological Studies. *Journal of Studies on Alcohol* **36** (7): 797-824.

Beck, A. (1974) The Development of Depression. In R. Friedman and M. Kurtz (eds), *The Psychology of Depression: Contemporary Research and Theory*. New York: Wiley.

Brown, G., and Harris, T. (1978) *Social Origins of Depression*. London: Tavistock Publications.

Brown, G., Bhrolchain, M., and Harris, T. (1975) Social Class and Psychiatric Disturbance among Women in an Urban Population. *Sociology* **9**: 225-254.

Cahalan, D. (1970) *Problem Drinkers*. San Francisco: Jossey-Bass Inc.

Cahalan, D. and Room, R. (1974) *Problem Drinking Among American Men*. New Brunswick: Rutgers Centre of Alcohol Studies.

Carlson, R. (1970) On the structure of Self-esteem: Comments on Ziller's Formulation. *Journal of Consulting and Clinical Psychology* 37: 264-268.

Cartwright, A., Shaw, S., and Spatley, T. (1975) *Designing a Comprehensive Community Response to Problems of Alcohol Abuse.* Report to the Department of Health and Social Security by the Maudsley Alcohol Pilot Project, London.

Castle, C. (1913) A Statistical Study of Eminent Women. *Archives of Psychology* 27: 42-8.

Child, I., Barry, H. III, and Bacon, M. (1965) A Cross-cultural Study of Drinking, *Quarterly Journal of Studies on Alcohol.* Supplement No. 3: 49-61.

Cloward, R. and Ohlin, L. (1960) *Delinquency and Opportunity.* New York: Free Press.

Costello, R. (1975) Alcoholism Treatment and Evaluation. In Search of Methods II. Collation of Two-Year follow-up Studies. *International Journal of Addictions* 10: 857-76.

Cotton, N. (1979) The Familial Incidence of Alcoholism. *Journal of Studies on Alcohol* 40 (1): 89-116.

Davies, J. and Stacey, B. (1972) *Teenagers and Alcohol: A Developmental Study in Glasgow.* Vol. II. London: HMSO.

Dight, S.E. (1976) *Scottish Drinking Habits.* London: HMSO.

Dweck, C. and Bush, E. (1976) Sex Differences in Learned Helplessness. I. Differential Debilitation with Peer and Adult Evaluators. *Developmental Psychology* 12: 147-156.

Dweck, C. and Repucci, N. (1973) Learned Helplessness and Reinforcement Responsibility in Children. *Journal of Personality and Social Psychology* 25: 109-116.

Edwards, G., Chandler, J., and Hensman, C. (1972) Drinking in a London Suburb. Correlates of Trouble with Drinking among Men (2) *Quarterly Journal of Studies on Alcohol.* Supplement No. 6: 94-119.

Edwards, G., Gross, M., Keller, M., Moser, J., and Room, R. (1977) *Alcohol Related Disabilities.* Geneva: WHO Offset Publication No. 32.

Ellis, H. (1904) *A Study of British Genius.* London: Hurst

Erikson, E. (1964) Inner and Outer Space: Reflections on Womanhood. *Daedalus* 93.

Gatchel, R. and Proctor, J. (1976) Physiological Correlates of

Learned Helplessness in Man. *Journal of Abnormal Psychology* **85**: 27-34.

Gomberg, E. (1976a) The Female Alcoholic. In R. Tarter and A. Sugerman (eds), *Alcoholism*. Massachusetts: Addison-Wesley Publishing Company.

—— (1976b) Alcoholism in Women. In B. Kissin and H. Begleiter (eds), *The Biology of Alcoholism*. Vol. 4. New York: Plenum Press.

Gove, W. (1972) The Relationship between Sex Roles, Marital Status and Mental Illness. *Social Forces* **51**: 34-44.

Gove, W. and Tudor, J. (1973) Adult Sex Roles and Mental Illness. *American Journal of Sociology* **78**: 812-835.

Hawker, A. (1978) *Adolescents and Alcohol*. London: Edsall.

Jacklin, C. and Mischel, H. (1973) As the Twig is Bent: Sex Role Stereotyping in Early Readers. *School Psychology Digest* **2** (3): 30-38.

Jahoda, G. and Crammond, J. (1972) *Children and Alcohol: a Developmental Study in Glasgow*. Vol. 1. London: HMSO.

Jessor, R., Graves, T., Hanson, R., and Jessor, S. (1968) *Society, Personality and Deviant Behaviour. A Study of a Tri-ethnic Community*. New York: Holt, Rhinehart and Winston.

Jones, M. (1971) Personality Antecedents and Correlates of Drinking Patterns in Women. *Journal of Consulting and Clinical Psychology*. **36**: 61-65.

Kaplan, H. (1973) Self-Derogation and Social Position: Interaction effects of Sex, Race, Education and Age. *Social Psychology* **8**: 92-99.

Karpman, B. (1948) *The Alcoholic Woman*. Washington: Linacre Press.

Keller, M. (1972) The Oddities of Alcoholics. *Quarterly Journal of Studies on Alcohol*. **33**: 1147-1148.

Knupfer, G. (1964) Female Drinking Patterns. In Selected papers presented at the fifteenth annual meeting of the North American Association of Alcoholism. Washington DC. Unpublished.

Levis, D. (1976) Learned Helplessness: A Reply and an Alternative S-R Interpretation. *Journal of Experimental Psychology* **105**: 47-65.

Lindbeck, B.L. (1972) The Woman Alcoholic. *International Journal of Addiction* **7**: 567-80.

Maccoby, E. and Jacklin, C. (1974) *The Psychology of Sex Differences.* Stanford: Stanford University Press.

Mesdag, M. (1979) *British Drink Profiles.* Colchester: Halliday Associates.

Miller, I. and Norman, W. (1979) Learned Helplessness in Humans. A Review and Attribution-Theory Model. *Psychological Bulletin* **86** (1): 93-118.

Miller, W. and Seligman, M. (1976) Learned Helplessness, Depression, and the Perception of Reinforcement. *Behaviour, Research and Therapy* **14**: 7-17.

Millett, K. (1972) *Sexual Politics.* London: Sphere Books.

O'Connor, J. (1978) *The Young Drinkers.* London: Tavistock Publications.

Parker, F. (1972) Sex Role Adjustment in Women Alcoholics. *Quarterly Journal of Studies on Alcohol* **33**: 647-657.

Plant, M. (1979) *Drinking Careers.* London: Tavistock Publications.

Raskin, A. and Golob, R. (1966) Occurrence of Sex and Social Class Differences in Premorbid Competence, Symptom and Outcome Measures in Acute Schizophrenia. *Psychological Reports* **18**: 11-22.

Rheingold, J. (1964) *The Fear of Being a Woman.* New York: Grune & Stratton.

Riviere, J. (1959) (ed.) *Collected Papers of Sigmund Freud.* New York: Basic Books.

Rohsenow, D. and O'Leary, M. (1978) Locus of Control. Research on Alcoholic populations: A Review. *International Journal of the Addictions* **13** (1): 55-78.

Sangree, W. (1962) The Social Functions of Beer Drinking In Bantu Tiriki. In D. Pittman and C. Snyder (eds), *Society, Culture and Drinking Patterns.* New York: John Wiley and Sons.

Saunders, W. and Kershaw P. (1978) The Prevalence of Drinking and Alcoholism in the West of Scotland. *British Journal of Psychiatry* **133**: 493-99.

Schuckit, M., Pitts, F., and Reich, T. (1969) Alcoholism: Two Types of Alcoholism in Women. *Archives of General Psychiatry* **20**: 301-306.

Schuckit, M. (1972) The Alcoholic Woman: A Literature Review. *Psychiatry in Medicine* **3**: 37.

Sciada, J. and Vannicelli, M. (1978) Sex Role Conflict and Women's Drinking. *Journal of Studies on Alcohol* **10** (1): 28-44.

Sclare, A. (1970) The Female Alcoholic. *British Journal of Addictions* **65**: 99-107.

Seligman, M. (1975) *Helplessness: On depression, Development and Death*. San Francisco: Freeman.

Skog, O. (1973) Less Alcohol – fewer Alcoholics. *The Drinking and Drug Practices Surveyor* **7**: 7-13.

Wanberg, K. and Horn, J. (1970) Alcoholism Symptom Patterns of Men and Women: A Comparative Study. *Quarterly Journal of Studies on Alcohol* **31**: 40-61.

Weiner, B., Nierenberg, R., and Goldstein, M. (1976) Social Learning (Locus of Control) versus Attributional (Causal Stability) Interpretations of Expectancy of Success. *Journal of Personality* **44**: 52-68.

Weissman, M. and Klerman, G. (1977) Sex Differences and the Epidemiology of Depression. *Archives of General Psychiatry* **34**: 98-111.

Weisstein, N. (1977) Psychology Constructs the Female. In J. English (ed.), *Sex Equality*. New Jersey: Prentice-Hall.

Wilsnack, S. (1973) Sex Role Identity in Female Alcoholism. *Journal of Abnormal Psychology* **82**: 253-61.

Winokur, G. and Clayton, P. (1967) Family History Studies II. Sex Differences and Alcoholism in Primary Affective Illness. *British Journal of Psychiatry* **113**: 973-79.

Worrell, J. (1978) Sex Roles and Psychological Well-being Perspective on Methodology. *Journal of Consulting and Clinical Psychology* **46** (4): 777-791.

5

CLARE WILSON

Research Psychologist
Addiction Research Unit
London

The family

It is forty years since the first reports on wives of alcoholics were published. Since then interest in the family of the alcoholic has increased steadily and numerous research and clinical papers have appeared about the partners and children of excessive drinkers. However, very few of these papers concern women drinkers and their families and, whilst it has become something of a cliché to speak about alcoholism as a 'family problem', very little of the research or clinical literature explicitly considers the whole family and the way in which alcohol fits into the total pattern of family behaviour. Given this dearth of information on maternal drinking problems and their impact on the family, this chapter must necessarily be somewhat speculative. It attempts to draw together salient themes from the largely separate bodies of literature on women with drinking problems, the family and marital interaction of excessive drinkers, and the impact of parental drinking on children. In so doing, it must grapple with the lack of fit between concepts used in these separate areas of study and is often faced with a complete lack of information as to whether processes that are important in understanding the family life of male drinkers are applicable in the case of women.

Lindbeck (1972: 578) identified 'the spouse of the female alcoholic and the role he plays in the development of her problem and its progression and her attitude toward seeking help' and 'the effect of the alcoholic mother on her children', as two areas especially neglected in the literature on women and alcohol. Why should there be this neglect? It may be that it represents yet another example of the general tendency for researchers to regard the male drinker as a more important subject for study than his female counterpart. Yet there may also be rather deeper 'motivations' behind the lack of research on women drinkers in relation to their families.

As discussed in chapter 4, a powerful element in the negative social stereotype of the woman alcoholic is the strong emotional reaction to the idea that a drunken woman cannot properly care for her children and provide a secure, stable home for the family. The centrality of the roles of wife and mother in our society requires that behaviour, such as drinking, which threatens to diminish the capacity of women to fulfill these roles will be met with strong social sanctions aimed at controlling it. There is a belief that it is worse for children to have a mother who drinks heavily than a father who is a problem drinker; this is frequently expressed in more speculative articles. For example, two articles on the children of alcoholics discuss the situation of children with drinking mothers in single paragraphs as quoted below:

> 'Literature relating to the alcoholic mother is not abundant. However, Fox has stated that when a mother is alcoholic, the children suffer irreparable damage. The inconsistent show of affection for the children produces long-lasting feelings of rejection, abandonment, and isolation.' (Sloboda, 1974: 606)

> '(If it is the mother who is the alcoholic, the situation is even more desperate. Children, especially young children, are more dependent on their mother. Obviously alcoholic mothers cannot care for either their children's physical or emotional needs).' (Bosma, 1972: 34. Parentheses in original.)

It is not just the commentators who hold this belief; women drinkers have also internalized the idea that it is worse for the mother to drink.

> 'My head tells me I'm sick, my head tells me it's no worse, no

better than a man who drinks heavily, but my heart still tells me it's worse. I'm not just a person who has a drink problem – I'm a mother who boozes and that must be evil. But a man who drinks, even a father, well, that's just the way of the world'. (Burnie, Cosmopolitan, 1979).

Perhaps the threat posed by alcohol abuse to our idealized notions of women's place in the family and the social stereotype which acts so powerfully to control women's drinking are sufficiently strongly felt by all of us that we prefer to accept the belief that a woman who drinks excessively must be a more damaging influence than a man with a drinking problem, rather than to demand empirical study of the respective influences of men and women drinkers in their families. It is perhaps as well to examine our own attitudes when considering both themes from research and treatment for women drinkers with families.

Marital relationships

Divorce and separation have been consistently found to be more common among problem drinkers than among control or comparison groups (Bailey, 1961; Moss and Beresford-Davies, 1967; Ablon, 1976) and marital conflict is frequently reported by problem drinkers (Cahalan, 1970). National Institute on Alcohol Abuse and Alcoholism, 1971). With the development of an interactional approach to alcohol problems, disfunctional family interaction has been implicated in the initiation and maintenance of excessive drinking and researchers have begun to focus on marital conflict as a major area of family disfunction. Research on the nature and effects of marital conflict has, however, focused only on men with drinking problems and has largely ignored children and families where the wife is the drinker.

Whilst we thus have little information about the effects of marital conflict on the woman drinker's family, the theme of marital and sexual adjustment has figured quite prominently in the literature on women alcoholics. Marital conflict is frequently cited by women as a reason for starting to drink heavily (e.g. Lisansky, 1957; Rosenbaum, 1958) or for seeking help (Sclare, 1970). However, there is no evidence that conflict is more severe or more prevalent in the marriages of women drinkers than those of their male counterparts. It may be that marital conflict assumes a greater salience for women, given the social position of many women as full-time wives and mothers and the social conditioning that still leads them to identify themselves through these roles. This hypothesis gains some credibility from the fact that men tend to cite events such as financial problems or loss of a job as reasons for seeking help – factors which may be salient in men's self-definition. However, Dahlgren (1975), commenting on the finding that women, more often than men, tend to cite an external event or circumstance as the precipitant of heavy drinking, suggests that the greater social stigma attached to heavy drinking by women leads them to feel more need to find a justification for their drinking than do men. Thus men and women problem drinkers may, perhaps, share similar experiences of troubled marriages but may place different emphasis on their marital difficulties as a result of their different social positions.

Another issue of importance in considering the quality of the marital relationships of women problem drinkers is the finding that many of these women are married to men who are themselves heavy or problem drinkers. The majority of studies report higher rates of problem drinking among these men than among men in the general population (Jacob *et al.*, 1978). Problem drinking is also more common among husbands of women drinkers than among wives of men who drink excessively (Gomberg, 1976). Some women begin to drink with their husbands, either socially or in an effort to exert control over the man's consumption (Orford *et al.*, 1975) and may become addicted in the process (Gomberg, 1974). Rosenbaum (1958: 87) reported that a majority of the husbands of her women patients were excessive drinkers and that 'in a majority of cases, the husband's own drinking, as well as his nonconstructive attitude towards the wife's drinking were cited as major areas of conflict in the marital relationship'. Marriage to an excessive drinker may thus be a cause of both heavy drinking and poor marital relationships for many women and may be more characteristic of women problem drinkers than it is of men.

Whilst drinking may be a focus of conflict in families with drinking problems it is often not the only, or even the most important, subject of arguments. Wilson and Orford (1978) found that rows often centred on other subjects such as money, sexual relationships, child care, or one partner's fussy or demanding behaviour in families of both men and women with drinking problems.

Researchers have suggested that marital conflict may constitute one of the more important mediators of the impact of parental drinking on children (Booz-Allen and Hamilton, 1974). Children may often be present during parental rows and may intervene to try and separate their parents, or may become involved on the side of one of the partners. Parental arguments may be more upsetting for children than the drinking: one study (Cork, 1969) found that ninety-eight of 115 children interviewed said that 'parental fighting and quarrelling' was their 'main concern', whilst six children said drunkenness, and only one child drinking, was their main concern. Children who are very withdrawn in school may be worried or fearful because of parental fighting, or just tired because they have been kept awake by arguments at night. Some children say they are unable to concentrate in school because they are worried about events in the family and others cannot do their homework in peace because of parental arguments. It is possible that some of the negative consequences suffered by children from problem drinking families, for example, underachievement, conduct problems, and poor school performance (e.g. Chafetz *et al.*, 1971; Kammeier, 1971; Cork, 1969; Parnitzke and Prüssing, 1966) may originate from marital conflict rather than parental drinking *per se*.

Family violence

Alcoholism and heavy drinking have been related both to wife beating (Gayford, 1975; Marsden and Owens, 1975; Scott, 1974) and child abuse and neglect (Mayer and Black, 1977; Stewart, 1970). However, there are many conflicting findings among research reports in this area and we are still a long way from being clear about the exact relationships between drinking, drunkenness, alcohol abuse, and family violence. Only a few studies of families in which child abuse or neglect has occurred have attempted to examine the extent to which alcohol and drug abuse is involved. Similarly, the alcohol literature is imprecise when it comes to defining 'conflict' and there has been little specific research on family violence in alcohol-abusing families.

Mayer and Black (1977) note that many of the child character-istics, situations, and personality factors which have been asso-ciated with child abuse and neglect are also found in families with alcohol problems. Young (1964), reviewing 300 case histo-ries of families where children had been abused or neglected, found that drinking was a 'primary family problem' in 62 per cent of the families and that heavy drinking was present but not the main problem, in additional families. Fitch (1975) reported that 32 per cent of child abusers – 41 per cent of fathers and 10 per cent of mothers – used alcohol disfunctionally. Among neglected children – children who failed to thrive – significantly more fathers of these children had a drinking problem than fathers of abused children. On the other hand, Steele and Pollock (1968) interviewed sixty families of abused children from a variety of socio-economic backgrounds and found only one family where a psychiatric diagnosis of 'alcoholism' could be made.

It may be that intoxication, rather than 'alcoholism', could be the precipitating factor in child abuse (El-Guebaly and Offord, 1977) or that drinking problems are more strongly related to child neglect than to child abuse (Mayer and Black, 1977). These questions are among many which remain unanswered:

> 'The importance of clarifying terminology and the need for controlled studies designed to unravel the possible etiologic relationships among alcoholism, poverty, family disorganisa-tion, and battering are clear. It is an open question whether alcoholism is causally related to child battering or whether both alcoholism and battering arise from common factors present in these families.' (El-Guebaly and Offord, 1977: 358-9)

A similar lack of clarity exists in the relationship between drinking and violence towards the marital partner, although there is little doubt that the two frequently occur together. A study in America (Byles, 1978) found a significant association between alcohol problems and violence among persons seeking help from a family court. Gayford (1975) studied 100 battered women and found that in forty-four cases beatings occurred only after the man had been drinking. In fifty-two cases the woman's husband drank heavily at least once a week. Orford and co-workers (1976) in a study of 100 male alcoholics and their wives found that seventy-two of the women had been threatened by their husbands and forty-five had been beaten. There is some evidence that women who are beaten by their partners may begin to drink heavily in reaction to the beatings (Marsden and Owens, 1975; Wilson and Orford, 1978). It also seems that women who drink excessively may be attacked by their partner because of their drinking (Rosenbaum, 1958).

Children are likely to be affected by parental violence, whether or not they are physically abused themselves. They may intervene in fights, be involved in attending to injuries or cleaning up after a row. Some children may stay away from school or not go out to visit friends in order to try and prevent a parental argument or to protect a parent (Wilson and Orford, 1978).

Research has indicated that persons who are violent towards their marital partners and/or children have often experienced violence in their childhood homes (Renvoize, 1978). It is likely that children brought up by violent parents model their behaviour on this example and learn that violence may be an effective means to control others or to express feelings of frustration or hostility. Some of the children I interviewed said that they had been violent towards one of their parents, usually the drinker. Some attack their drinking parent in order to protect the non-drinker whilst others use violence as a way of releasing pent-up emotions. This seems to be equally common among children of both male and female drinkers. Younger children sometimes report feelings of frustration and helplessness because they are not strong enough to stand up to an aggressive parent or to protect one parent from the violence of the other.

One study (Keane and Roche, 1974), which used a clear operational definition of violence, found that the presence of a violent alcoholic father was related to symptoms of developmental disorder in both boys and girls aged ten years. Boys – but not girls – with an alcoholic father showed a greater number of symptoms of developmental disorder than controls. Among children with alcoholic fathers, both boys and girls whose fathers were also violent showed significantly more symptoms than those whose drinking fathers were not violent. These results indicate that violence accompanying paternal drinking is likely to have a particularly severe impact on children, but there is no equivalent research on the effects of violence by mothers with drinking problems.

Family communication

Family conflict and violence may be seen as one manifestation of problems with communication among family members. Clinical and research observations indicate that communication in families with alcohol problems is often circular and non-productive, consisting of a large proportion of nagging, bickering, sarcastic comments, and sharp rebukes (Paolino and McCrady, 1977). It is not uncommon to find that the whole family rarely talks together and that family members find difficulty in giving direct expression of needs, dissatisfactions, or appreciation.

Patterns of communication may alter depending on whether the drinker is drunk or sober. This has been demonstrated in a series of studies by Steinglass and co-workers (Steinglass, Weiner, and Mendelson, 1971; Davis *et al.*, 1974; Steinglass, 1977) in which they observed groups of family members on a hospital ward. The families were initially observed while the drinker was sober and had no access to alcohol. In a second stage the drinker was allowed unlimited access to alcohol and the family members' behaviour observed during drinking and intoxication. The behaviour of each family member was seen to change during the second, drinking, stage, and these changes occurred in a consistent fashion over subsequent observations of the family in the sober and drinking conditions. The researchers give the example of a family which was stiff, reserved, and relatively silent when the father was sober, but laughed, joked and talked in an animated fashion while he was drinking. They suggest that drinking can serve a particular function for a family: in the example given, the father's drunkenness gave 'permission' for each member to communicate things in a light-hearted, joking manner which they could not express in the sober state.

While this family's ability to communicate openly was

increased by drinking, in other families the reverse is often the case. In two families observed by the author (in both of which the woman was the drinker), family communication was severely curtailed during episodes of drinking. In each family the woman would be drinking in a room on her own, away from the rest of the family, and other family members would keep their distance by, for example, going to their bedrooms or sitting around the television. In each family, communication among the non-drinking members would be almost non-existent and an atmosphere of silence and tension characterized the whole household. Both these women said that part of the reason they drank heavily was because they felt unable to cope with pressures in the family, particularly the demands and expectations of their husbands. In each case, the reaction of the family was such that they were, in effect, given a respite from family pressures.

In families where the man is the problem drinker he may become isolated because communication between him and other family members becomes attenuated. In several families interviewed by the author the mother and children appeared to have formed a fairly close 'coalition' which excluded the drinking father. In some this 'coalition' persisted whether the man was drinking or sober, whilst in others it would be relaxed and some degree of communication established with the drinker when he stopped drinking. We formed the impression that women drinkers may be isolated, ignored or rejected by their families during drinking episodes, but that no equivalent 'coalition' exists between father and children and that the woman's isolation ends when she sobers up. This is a tenuous suggestion, based on observations of a small number of cases but, if replicated in a larger sample, it might have the important implication that children may maintain a stronger relationship with a drinking mother than a drinking father and perhaps suffer less from the type of parental loss which has been held to characterize children of problem drinkers.

Parent-child relationships

Specific patterns of parent-child relationships have been described in the literature as though they were characteristic of all families experiencing drinking problems (e.g. Newell, 1950; Mik, 1970). However, other workers have made it clear that a variety of patterns of parent-child relationships occur in different families and between different children and their parents within the same family (Cork, 1969; Wilson and Orford, 1978). Some children show fairly consistent positive or negative attitudes to one or both parents, others may be ambivalent about them. The quality of children's attitudes towards their parents may vary according to whether the drinking parent is sober or intoxicated. For example, the drinker may be rejected while s/he is drinking and the children may also withdraw from the non-drinking parent if s/he is perceived as behaving oversolicitously towards the drinker at these times. As in all families siblings may react differently to their parents and parents often find some children easier to relate to than others.

A study from Canada (McLachlan, Walderman, and Thomas, 1973) constitutes our most comprehensive empirical knowledge of parent-child relationships in families of men and women with drinking problems and of the influence of the parent's recovery on these relationships. Fifty-four adolescent children of unrecovered and recovered problem drinkers and an equal number of control children were interviewed and given measures of personality, drug and alcohol use, perceived social distance from parents, perceived social competence, and family harmony. There were no differences between any of the groups in their use of alcohol or other drugs, school performance or personality measures, although children of problem drinkers had lower self-esteem than controls.

Teenagers with unrecovered drinking fathers rated themselves as more socially distant from their fathers than did controls, whilst there was no difference for children of recovered fathers and controls, nor between children of recovered mothers or unrecovered mothers and controls. This suggests that adolescents see themselves as distant from an actively drinking father, whilst this is not the case for those with drinking mothers. A similar pattern was found for ratings of social competence: unrecovered fathers received a very low rating, whilst there were no significant differences between the groups in ratings of the social competence of their mothers. Problem drinkers' children rated their families lower on family harmony than controls, and those with unrecovered mothers and fathers rated their families as less cohesive than those whose drinking parents had recovered. The ratings were lowest for families where the father was actively drinking, intermediate for families with both actively drinking and recovered mothers, and highest for those with recovered fathers, which were given as high a rating as controls.

The authors caution that this sample was too small for any great confidence to be placed on the results. However, the findings suggest that there may be better relationships between adolescent children and their problem drinking mothers than with actively drinking fathers and that there may be less family harmony when the father is the actively drinking parent.

Family roles

The allocation and performance of family roles has been a major focus of attention from researchers interested in the impact of stress in the family: changes in family role playing have been investigated in studies of families facing a range of crises including unemployment, war, bereavement (Hill and Hansen, 1962) and alcoholism (Jackson, 1954; Lemert, 1960). A main assumption of these studies is that when one family member ceases to play his/her allocated roles within the family, other members must take over the vacant role positions if the family unit is to continue to function. Taking on additional role responsibility may place a strain on the individual concerned which can lead to symptoms of physical and psychological disorder. Thus role changes, increased role responsibility, and the failure of family members to take on vacant role positions are important factors mediating the impact of a crisis such as alcoholism on family members.

Work with the wives of alcoholics has demonstrated that these women assume increasing responsibility for family roles as their husbands become progressively unable to perform the tasks which were previously their responsibility:

'The wife . . . usually begins to ease her husband out of his family roles. She assumes husband and father roles. This involves strengthening her role as mother and putting aside her role as wife. She becomes the manager of the home, the discipliner of the children, the decision-maker.' (Jackson, 1954: 576).

In many cases the wife will assume the role of bread-winner and be working full-time outside the home as well as taking full responsibility for domestic management and the care of the children. Not surprisingly, wives in this position are frequently exhausted, physically and emotionally, and may show a number of symptoms of physical or psychological disturbance.

A number of studies have examined the process of adjustment by wives of alcoholics to their husband's excessive drinking and the strategies they adopt in trying to cope (Jackson, 1954; Lemert, 1960; Orford *et al.*, 1975; James and Goldman, 1971). However, there is no comparable research on the adjustment and coping styles adopted by husbands of women with drink problems.

The author's observational work with families of excessive drinkers has suggested that in cases where the pattern of drinking is one of steady tippling through the day, and does not involve incapacitating intoxication, the drinker is capable of carrying out most of the routine household chores. This observation applied to women who worked full-time in the home and to a few cases where unemployed men took responsibility for the domestic tasks while their wives worked full-time outside the home. In these cases the drinker would usually be relatively sober when their partner and children returned home and an evening meal would be prepared for the whole family (Wilson and Orford, 1978).

Where the drinking pattern involves a greater degree of intoxication, the ability of the drinker to perform these household tasks is correspondingly diminished. In such cases there may be more necessity for other members of the family to take over household tasks. The provision of an evening meal often seems to be a focus of resentment and dissatisfaction: many husbands complained that the dinner was often not prepared or was spoiled and seemed to resent strongly having to make a meal for themselves and their children.

Taking control of the purse strings is a role usually assumed by the non-drinking partner at a relatively early stage in the development of drinking problems in an effort to cut down or block access to alcohol. This means of control probably involves a lesser degree of role change where the wife is the drinker, as it is more usual for women to be economically dependent on their husbands. In many families the drinker's husband will take responsibility for shopping, either doing it himself, or with a child, or accompanying his wife on shopping trips. In some families, the wife is given an allowance to cover shopping which is not enough to allow spending on alcohol and may sometimes have to present detailed accounts of all her purchases.

The children of problem drinkers may assume a considerable weight of responsibility for tasks within the family. They may assume tasks directly from the drinker, or they may take on some of the non-drinker's roles when the non-drinker assumes more of the drinker's former responsibilities. Demands that children take on responsibility which is too heavy or inappropriate for their age or stage of development may have negative consequences for the child's development.

Cork (1969) found that many of the children she interviewed took responsibility for household tasks and the author's work has shown the same results. Many children take on a relatively large share of chores such as washing up, cleaning, preparing food and cups of tea, answering the telephone and buying the odd item from local shops. Most of the children I have interviewed do not express resentment or appear upset at having to do these jobs; in most cases the amount of chores they were expected to do seemed no more onerous than those normally asked of children. It could even be argued that, when the tasks are not too demanding, this measure of responsibility and the need to acquire certain skills could be a useful experience for the children.

On the other hand, children in families with drinking problems may be asked to take on roles that make emotional demands or involve stressful experiences that are inappropriate for the child's stage of emotional maturity. One such role is caring for younger siblings. Cork (1969: 25-6) reports that some older children: 'felt an unusual degree of responsibility towards the younger ones – not only for their physical care, but also for their emotional development. Many tried, without much success, to prepare the younger children for the problems they themselves were facing.'

Whilst some of the younger children had 'relatively close relationships with older brothers or sisters who gave them care and attention', others resented the parental role assumed by the older ones. Some older children also felt resentment at having to act like parents to their younger siblings and Cork noted that for a number 'the apparent need to dominate their juniors was probably a result of deep feelings of aggression or frustration'.

Very similar patterns have been observed by the author and appear to occur in the families of both male and female drinkers. Where the father is the drinking parent, older children are more likely to have to look after younger ones if their mother is working outside the home or if there is a very large family. It may be that where the mother is the drinker children are required more often to take responsibility for their younger siblings.

Whilst heavy social sanctions are directed at excessive drinkers, particularly women, for the neglect of their children, it is quite clear from the literature that the nature of role changes in the family of the excessive drinker can be such that *both* parents fail to perform adequately their parental roles. It is frequently reported that children may feel closer to the drinking than the non-drinking parent and may feel more rejected by the non-drinking mother or father who is perceived as too busy, too wrapped up in his or her own troubles, or too preoccupied with the drinker to care about the children. As Fox (1962: 87) suggests: 'How each parent plays his [sic] various roles will determine to a great extent the child's future mental health.'

The argument has been that maternal drinking problems have a direct effect upon the development of children, particularly younger children, where their helplessness requires constant adult attention, and the fulfilment of their need for close, symbiotic ties with the mother figure is important for the development of a stable self-concept, sense of security, and trust in others. Excessive drinking by the father is perceived as having a less direct effect on the development of the young child but, as Fox has pointed out, the disruption of the infant's close ties with the mother may be as complete as if the mother herself were drinking:

'The effects of an alcoholic father on young children may be more indirect than direct. If the mother is loving and relaxed the child will thrive, but if she is neurotic herself, or angry or exhausted, hostile and worried, the child will suffer. Even her milk can disagree with the infant at such a time. The tension she feels will infect her child and there will be a serious disturbance of the empathy between them. If this negative state lasts too long, the development of the child's ego can be seriously interfered with. Because of an overwhelming disappointment in a marriage, some mothers will reject their children, especially if they happen to look or act like the father. They are apt to become over-solicitous with these children because of their guilt feelings. Others will turn to the children for a satisfaction of all their love needs, pushing the alcoholic father completely out of the picture.' (Fox, 1962: 86).

In sum, it would appear that the impact of changes or inadequacies in parental role-playing may depend less upon the sex of the drinker and the tasks that are considered appropriate for males and females respectively than upon the adjustment that the non-drinking parent can make, the adequacy with which s/he copes with the problems posed by the partner's drinking, and the nature and weight of responsibilities borne by the children. Over-challenging emotional demands and a lack of physical and emotional support from the non-drinking parent are likely to have deleterious consequences for the child's emotional and social development.

Social isolation

In the early stages of development of drinking problems, both the drinker and spouse will collude together to deny that anything is wrong and that drinking is inappropriate. Excuses, such as 'she didn't realize how many times her glass was being filled up' or 'he was under such a lot of pressure' are offered and accepted. Denial and rationalization may continue well past the point where it is obvious to both partners that episodes of drunkenness are becoming increasingly frequent and are beginning to cause embarrassment both to the couple and to their friends and relatives. At this point the couple can become increasingly socially isolated: they may stop going out to avoid embarrassment and friends may stop asking them to functions where alcohol is served, or make excuses to avoid visiting the home.

This pattern of isolation, imposed from within and outside the family, occurs for both male and female drinkers, but where the drinker is female, self-imposed isolation and efforts to conceal her drinking may be more pronounced than is the case for men. Women who start to drink heavily at home very often show a pattern of carefully concealed, secret drinking. By confining their drinking to the early part of the day, avoiding extreme intoxication, sobering up before the family comes home and removing or hiding bottles, women may be able to hide their drinking from their family for some considerable period. When the drinking is discovered, women are likely to continue trying to hide and deny it and are certainly unlikely to expose the fact to persons outside the family.

The greater stigma attached to heavy drinking and drunkenness in women produces strong feelings of shame in every member of the family. Not only is the woman reluctant to expose herself to social censure, but her husband is likely to try and keep his wife's drinking a closely guarded secret. This is not only to protect the woman and children, but also because a drinking wife is felt to reflect badly on his own masculine image and his ability to control his wife's behaviour. He may not only try to conceal the drinking from family, friends, and neighbours, but he may forbid his wife to consult the GP or other outside agencies for help with her drinking problems. It is also unlikely that he will approach agencies which might give help for problems experienced by himself or the children. If he does consult outside agencies, it is unlikely that he will mention his wife's drinking as a possible cause of the family problems.

Both parents may try to hide excessive drinking from the children, particularly younger children. The drinker's unusual behaviour is often explained as 'illness' to conceal its real nature. However, even very young children are usually aware that what is happening in the family is quite different from their usual experience of illness and may be worried and confused about it. When they discover the real explanation, children may be sworn to secrecy by the non-drinking parent for fear that they may tell neighbours or family friends. This injunction is usually strictly observed and often unnecessary: most children are acutely aware of the mystery and anxiety surrounding the alcohol-related behaviour and are very reluctant to risk exposing the dark family secret, even if they are not fully aware of the social stigma and associated attitudes of ostracism and rejection.

Children may thus feel unable to share their experience with peers or with adults, and are left to deal with their feelings of anxiety, fear, hostility, anger, and so on with no avenue of expression and possible relief. They often do not want to invite their friends home as they are afraid of being ashamed of their parent or rejected when their friends discover the parental drinking problem. Some children will not play outside with friends for fear their parent may come home drunk and others refuse to visit friends because they feel they cannot reciprocate the invitation. Occasionally, a friendship will end when the friend's parents find out about the drinking and forbid their child to continue the friendship.

The negative social stereotypes of the woman alcoholic are held by children as well as adults: 'Most of the children whose mothers were alcoholic said that mothers – or women in general – should not drink. Even those children who said "It's alright for Dad to drink," felt that mother's drinking was "disgusting – not like a mother." ' (Cork, 1969: 31)

Problems of social isolation, feelings of shame about the family, fear of rejection by friends, and other outsiders, and difficulties in making and keeping friendships are problems common to children with mothers or fathers who drink excessively. However, the greater social stigma attached to women's heavy drinking may lead to even more intense problems for children with drinking mothers.

Drinking pattern

There are striking differences in the drinking patterns of individual problem drinkers. However, the literature on alcohol and the family largely ignores these differences and discusses the impact of excessive drinking on the family with an apparent assumption that 'alcoholism' entails a self-explanatory behavioural entity. The author's work suggests, though, that the pattern of drinking strongly influences the family process and that knowledge of this pattern may be essential to an under-standing of the situation of family members.

Apart from differences in drinking pattern shown by indivi-duals, there are gross differences between men and women in their characteristic drinking patterns. The literature describes a typical pattern of women drinking at home, alone, and often tippling steadily throughout the day, only rarely becoming intoxicated to the point of losing control or being unable to do their housework (Lindbeck, 1972; Lisansky, 1957; Gomberg, 1974; Dahlgren, 1978). On the other hand, men more typically drink in company, out of the home and may be more likely to become very drunk on each drinking occasion. Obviously, there are exceptions: some women drink outside the home and return in an incapable condition, others become very drunk and may be violent at home. Similarly, some men drink only at home and some unemployed men may show drinking patterns very similar to the steady tippling pattern shown by women.

The pattern of drinking and its associated behaviour obviously has a profound influence on family process. For instance, the drinker's ability to perform family roles, and thus the extent of role changes within the family, will depend greatly on the frequency of intoxication, the time of day when drinking occurs, and the extent to which drunkenness is incapacitating. The child-ren's exposure to drinking and drunkenness will likewise vary according to the parental drinking pattern. Where the parent returns home in an incapable, aggressive, or depressed state, the children may be fearful and apprehensive as a result. Where the parent does not get very drunk, the children may be less afraid or upset by the drinking, although they may still disapprove of it quite strongly. The amount of marital conflict or violence may similarly depend upon the frequency of drunken episodes, the presence or absence of aggressive moods accompanying drinking or drunken-ness, or the ability of the drinker to perform tasks within the family.

Help for the families of women with alcohol problems

Factors of special importance in the recognition of and response to drinking problems among women are discussed in detail in chapters 6 and 7. This section will therefore deal only with factors that are of particular relevance in the context of the families of women drinkers.

There is no research that examines help-seeking by husbands of women with drinking problems, although there are a number of papers that look at help-seeking by wives of male drinkers (e.g. Jackson and Kogan, 1963; Ablon, 1974; Hunter, 1963). This lack of information may be due not so much to a lack of interest on the part of researchers as a tendency for husbands of women problem drinkers not to approach community agencies for assistance with their own or family problems. Hunter (1963) notes that alcohol problems were involved in 21 per cent of cases presented to a family service agency in America, but that virtually none involved excessive drinking by a woman. Similarly, Ablon (1974) notes the small numbers of male Al-Anon members and suggests that men are reluctant to attend meetings if they will be the only male present. She also notes that the 'dearth of male spouses reflects the fact that men are more likely to walk out of a marriage where there is an alcoholic wife than are women in this situation with an alcoholic husband' (Ablon, 1974: 32).

In general, outside help tends to be sought only when attempts to solve the problem within the family have been repeatedly unsuccessful over a considerable period of time:

'As would be anticipated in a culture which places a high value on family self-sufficiency, most families first sought to use intra-family resources to deal with the problem of alcoholism, turning to extra-family resources some years after the excessive nature of the drinking was recognized.' (Jackson and Kogan, 1963: 467)

With their masculine image at stake and the social stigma surrounding drinking problems in women, it is probable that male partners of excessive drinkers are even more reluctant than their female counterparts to seek outside help for family problems. Ablon (1974: 33) noted that among families of male drinkers: 'The actual search for help for the alcoholic frequently was stimulated by a medical crisis or delinquent acting-out on the part of the children.'

The occurrence of a crisis may allow for a more 'acceptable' definition of the problem, in terms of 'sickness' for instance, and thus facilitate help-seeking by removing some of the feared stigma from the family. There is some evidence that women problem drinkers are more likely than men to be admitted to hospital as emergency cases following an acute crisis (Dahlgren and Myrhed, 1977). This study also showed that women were more often brought forcibly to the hospital by their husbands or other family members than were male drinkers. One can perhaps speculate that some men try to cope with their wives' drinking within the family and, when this is no longer possible, they place the blame for family problems on the woman's drinking and insist that she goes into treatment as the only solution for the difficulties.

The children of problem drinkers are very badly off when it comes to getting help for the problems they may experience as a consequence of parental drinking:

> 'In general, resources to meet the needs of these children are sadly lacking. Those community agencies and individuals which might logically be expected to help the children of alcoholic parents are too often not aware of the problem, much less geared to provide help. And because of the nature of the illness of alcoholism and its social stigma, the child is seldom able to actively seek help. Without the aid or intervention of helping persons, a child's access to the limited available resources is itself limited.' (Hindman, 1975: 2)

There has always been concern that the children of alcoholics constitute a group with a high risk of developing alcohol problems. A recent review calculated that about one third of adult problem drinkers had a parent (usually the father) with drinking problems (Cotton, 1979). This concern has been heightened in the present climate of worry about heavy drinking among teenagers. Rather more recently there has also been a growing awareness of the emotional, social, and psychological adjustment problems experienced by children whose parents drink excessively.

However, it is still the case that many specialist alcohol treatment agencies tend not to offer any practical help or counselling to the children of their clients: children report that they feel left out of the treatment process, do not understand what is happening to their drinking parent in treatment, and would like to have the chance to talk with the treatment staff about their problems in the family and to be given more information about alcoholism (Wilson and Orford, 1978).

Agents working with children who have been referred for psychological or behaviour problems may not be aware of parental drinking problems and the possibility of drinking problems at home may not be considered by teachers, youth leaders, and other workers dealing with difficult children on a regular basis. Community agencies have been described by one American report as more of a potential than an actual resource for problem drinkers' children: in general, they were inaccessible, did not understand the children's problems and feelings, and were unhelpful (Booz-Allen and Hamilton, 1974).

In America, there has been a movement to establish programmes of alcohol education in schools which offer, as an adjunct to the general education programme, counselling, advice, and sometimes recreational activities to those children who want help with alcohol-related problems. In some cases these programmes not only provide help for the children, but also motivate their parents to seek treatment for drinking problems (Weir, 1970).

When behavioural or psychological problems are related to parental drinking problems, treatment of the child on an individual basis may be doomed to failure because the root cause of the child's difficulties – the drinking and its consequences in the family – will not be open to therapeutic intervention. An approach to the family and an attempt to involve parents as well as the child in treatment may be more efficient means of intervention. A project in America has begun using family therapy in the treatment of behaviour problems in children of excessive drinkers and has found that family treatment has resulted in earlier identification and treatment of parental drinking problems (Hindman, 1975).

There are a number of reasons to suppose that family treatment may be a useful means of extending help to women with drinking problems and to their families. First, as indicated above, the inclusion of the whole family in cases where the child is the 'identified patient' may not only lead to more effective help for the child's problems, but also offer the chance for early recognition and response to the woman's drinking problem. It may be that the woman, and the other members of her family, would be more willing to examine her drinking in this setting than in the context of a specialist alcoholism treatment service.

The second indication for involving the woman's family comes from relatively recent theory and practice advocating the use of family therapy for alcohol problems. Impetus for this development has come from both the alcohol field and from family therapists. Research on the families of problem drinkers made it evident that the relationship between the drinker and the family was not one-way, but that the family also affects the drinker and the course of drinking problems. Equally, the family can either help or interfere with the treatment process.

Family therapists have stressed the importance of the concept of homeostasis (Jackson, 1957) in family systems. An early article (Ewing and Fox, 1968: 87) on the use of family theory in alcoholism treatment viewed the alcoholic marriage as a 'homeostatic mechanism' which is:

'established . . . to resist change over long periods of time. The behaviour of each spouse is rigidly controlled by the other. As a result, an effort by one person to alter his typical role behavior threatens the family equilibrium and provokes renewed efforts by the spouse to maintain the status quo.'

From a systems theory perspective, excessive drinking is perpetuated as an integral part of family function and homeostasis. In order to control drinking, it is thus necessary to change the behaviour patterns that together constitute this mechanism. A logical corollary to this hypothesis is that change brought about by individual therapy of the drinker will increase resistance by the spouse as a result of the implied threat to the status quo. This resistance may sabotage the potential for therapeutic progress with the drinker, but may be avoided if the spouse is included in treatment that focuses on the whole family system.

It has frequently been suggested that husbands of women drinkers are more likely to be resistant to their partner's treatment than are wives of problem drinkers. For example:

'the writer has heard therapists remark that the subtle ways in which a husband may encourage his wife's drinking because she is more sexually responsive, because it relieves his guilt, because it makes him an object of sympathy, are, for a wide variety of reasons, constructive and destructive.' (Gomberg, 1976: 146)

Theoretically, then, it would be even more important to include these husbands in treatment in order to modify the system that had hitherto perpetuated the woman's excessive drinking.

As discussed in chapter 7, treatment for women with drinking problems may involve these women in making far-reaching changes in their behaviour and attitudes, which can have considerable implications for their relationships in the family. For women to be able to make these changes, and for the changes to have the desired effect, other persons in the family, particularly husbands, must understand what is involved and the reasons behind new behaviour and attitudes. They must be in agreement with the goals and willing to change their own behaviour to incorporate changed interpersonal relationships and family roles in the pattern of family functioning. For these reasons, involvement of the husband is considered crucial by some writers on treatment for women drinkers.

Many women referred for alcoholism treatment are married to excessive drinkers with problems (Lisansky, 1957; Rosenbaum, 1958; Dahlgren, 1978) which is a further indication for joint treatment of the couple's alcohol-related problems.

Women with alcohol problems are neglected yet again in the literature on the effectiveness of family therapy with problem drinkers. In a recent review of the literature Dinaburg, Glick, and Feigenbaum (1977: 247) write:

'An extensive search of the literature on alcoholism, women alcoholics, family therapy and marital therapy revealed a paucity of controlled material. There are few articles which focus on the alcoholic family as a vital internally coherent system. There is even less written when the "identified patient" is a woman.'

In general, no firm conclusions may be reached about the efficacy of the various types of family therapy that have been tried with problem drinking families:

'The existing literature leaves us with a sense of guarded optimism about the application of family therapy techniques in the treatment of alcoholism. Although every study we have mentioned concludes with an enthusiastic statement encouraging greater use of family therapy, it is also apparent that very little hard evidence exists at this point demonstrating either the efficacy of family therapy by itself or the comparative value of family therapy versus more traditional forms of therapy in the treatment of alcoholism.' (Steinglass, 1977: 292)

The 'sense of guarded optimism' is based on a number of findings that have emerged from studies of family treatment in alcoholism. Male drinkers tend to remain in group therapy for a longer period when their wives are attending a concurrent group for spouses (Ewing, Long, and Wenzel, 1961; Smith, 1969). There appears to be a considerable improvement in marital satisfaction and a reduction in marital problems (Gliedman *et al.*, 1956; Ewing, Long, and Wenzel, 1961; Smith, 1969). Improvement in drinking problems seems to be associated with improvement in marital relationships and more satisfactory family communication (Meeks and Kelly, 1970).

As we have seen, marital conflict and dissatisfaction are salient factors in the family process for problem drinkers of both sexes. However, domestic conflict may be even more important in the causation and maintenance of women's excessive drinking and thus the broadening of therapeutic goals to include improvement in marital satisfaction as well as a reduction of drinking may be particularly relevant in the treatment of women problem drinkers.

Despite the indications for family therapy, it may be difficult to obtain participation by the whole family. These difficulties may be greater in the case of women patients, given that their husbands are frequently resistent to any intervention. The definition of drinking problems as involving the whole family, whilst sometimes allowing relief from guilt and responsibility for the 'identified patient', may create an unacceptable level of guilt and confusion among other members of the family which makes them resistent to such a definition and hence to participation in treatment. On the other hand, an approach that is sympathetic towards the difficulties experienced by the rest of the drinker's family and offers examination of these alongside help for the drinker may be more acceptable. The use of concurrent groups for drinkers and their partners may encourage spouses to participate and enable them to realize how drinking, rather than being the major, or only source of family problems, is closely related to the whole pattern of family behaviour. Meeting with others in the same position may allow them to express pent-up feelings and gradually recognize how their behaviour may be permitting, or even encouraging, excessive drinking. Conjoint family therapy may then be possible in cases where further work on a particular family's problems seems appropriate.

Whatever mode of treatment is offered to women drinkers with families, there are a number of issues that should concern the helper. The first is the question of whether in-patient or out-patient care is more appropriate. Admission to hospital may be seen by a woman who is strongly invested in the role of wife and mother as a heavy blow to her identity and, perhaps as confirmation of and punishment for failure. This has to be balanced by the needs of the rest of the family. If the father is unwilling or unable to care for children while their mother is in hospital, and no substitute is available, they may have to be taken into care and the family will be fragmented. Some men, relieved of responsibility, may take this situation as a chance to leave. In any case, reconstitution of the family may pose problems on discharge.

Child care is not, however, only a problem for residential services. Attendance at any agency can pose problems for women with children. It is rare that services make any provision for child care, although such provision would not only be of immense benefit to many clients, but would also provide the opportunity for workers to meet children, assess whether they have problems as a result of parental drinking and offer them information, advice, support, and referral for specialist help if necessary.

From a different angle, women may begin to drink excessively because they feel unable to cope with the roles of wife and mother. In such cases, they may benefit from a period of residential care with the chance of a respite from the demands of domestic responsibility. Examination of the problems and perhaps training in parenting can be offered in a non-threatening manner in a secure environment. Training in parenting would be helpful for many families with alcohol problems where there is concern over the children: it is not as yet widely available, but could provide a focus for involving drinkers and their families in a therapeutic context which is less stigmatized than an alcoholism service and could have great potential for prevention as well as treatment of family disfunction and childhood problems.

Just as separation from children may be therapeutically beneficial, separation from the partner may also be a desirable treatment outcome in some cases. Our society places great value on the intact nuclear family – a value that is often grounded in sentiment rather than practicality. Professional workers are frequently extremely reluctant to consider the break-up of a family as a desirable goal. However, a woman who is being abused, physically or emotionally, by her partner may use alcohol to provide an easily accessible escape. Physical escape is often extremely difficult for a woman who must not only overcome personal and social attitudes and values concerning her failure and loss of status if she leaves the family, but must also face the harsh realities of economic dependence, shortage of housing, problems of employment, and difficulties with child care. Practical help with these problems and counselling concerned with the emotional adjustment necessary for women to leave their partners is needed to facilitate this process.

Conclusions

It is clear that we do not have a complete or coherent picture of the family life of women with drinking problems. Research on alcohol and the family has concentrated almost exclusively on men and has failed to integrate findings from the separate areas of study of the spouses, children, and family interaction of problem drinkers. Whilst work on women drinkers has pointed out the importance of family factors in the initiation of excessive drinking, this research has neglected to examine the evolution of drinking problems and family disfunction and has also failed to come to grips with how these processes interact to affect the life of the whole family.

Much of the literature suggests that features of family disfunction, such as marital conflict, poor parent-child relationships, changes in the family role playing, social isolation, and communication problems characterize the families of both women and men with drinking problems. However, the manifestation of these factors and their salience for family members may be influenced by social norms and attitudes: differences in the social positions of the sexes, the family roles of wives/mothers and husbands/fathers, and the greater social stigma attached to excessive drinking by women may differentially influence the family life of men and women problem drinkers.

The lack of definitive information makes it difficult to derive firm strategies for treatment of women drinkers and their families. However, the mother's role in child care is obviously a crucial factor which is often not given sufficient consideration at present. There are also indications that involvement of the husband in treatment may be particularly important, especially where the husband is himself a heavy drinker and may be experiencing problems.

Recent developments in the application of general systems theory and family theory to alcohol problems have provided theoretical guidelines by means of which studies of component parts of the family can be integrated in order to proceed with research on the whole family. In general, these developments appear to offer the most promising approach to consolidating our knowledge about alcohol problems in the family and developing appropriate responses to drinking and associated family problems. We must make sure that women with drinking problems are included in future.

References

Ablon, J. (1974) Al-Anon Family Groups: Impetus for Learning and Change through the Presentation of Alternatives. *American Journal of Psychotherapy* **29** (1): 30-45.

Ablon, J. (1976) Family Structure and Behaviour in Alcoholism: A Review of the Literature. In B. Kissin and H. Begleiter (eds), *The Biology of Alcoholism, Vol. 4. Social Aspects of Alcoholism*. New York: Plenum Press.

Bailey, M.B. (1961) Alcoholism and Marriage: A Review of Research and Professional Literature. *Quarterly Journal of Studies on Alcohol* **22** (1): 81-97.

Booz-Allen and Hamilton, Inc. (1974) An Assessment of the Needs and Resources for Children of Alcoholic Parents.

Prepared for the US National Institute on Alcohol Abuse and Alcoholism (Rep. No. PB-241-119). Springfield, VA: National Technical Information Service.

Bosma, W.G.H. (1972) Children of Alcoholics – A Hidden Tragedy. *Maryland State Medical Journal* 21(1): 34-36.

Burnie, J. (1979) Was that last drink really chic – or one too many? *Cosmopolitan* January.

Byles, J.A. (1978) Violence, Alcohol Problems and other Problems in Disintegrating Families. *Journal of Studies on Alcohol* 39(3): 551-553.

Cahalan, D. (1970) *Problem Drinkers: A National Survey*. San Francisco: Jossey-Bass.

Chafetz, M.E., Blane, H.T., and Hill, M.J. (1971) Children of Alcoholics: Observations in the Child Guidance Clinic. *Quarterly Journal of Studies on Alcohol* 32(3): 687-693.

Cork, R.M. (1969) *The Forgotten Children: A Study of Children with Alcoholic Parents*. Toronto: Alcoholism and Drug Research Foundation of Ontario.

Cotton, N.S. (1979) The Familial Incidence of Alcoholism: A Review. *Journal of Studies on Alcohol* 40(1): 89-116.

Dahlgren, L. (1975) Special Problems in Female Alcoholism. *British Journal of Addiction* 70 Suppl. No. 1: 18-24.

Dahlgren, L. (1978) Female Alcoholics: III Development and Pattern of Problem Drinking. *Acta psychiatrica scandinavica* 57: 325-5.

Dahlgren, L. and Myrhed, M. (1977) Female Alcoholics: I. Ways of Admission to the Alcoholic Patient. A Study with Special Reference to the Alcoholic Female. *Acta psychiatrica scandinavica* 56: 39-49

Davis, D., Berenson, D., Steinglass, P., and Davis, S. (1974) The Adaptive Consequences of Drinking. *Psychiatry* 37(3): 209-215.

Dinaburg, D., Glick, I.D., and Feigenbaum, E. (1977) Marital Therapy of Women Alcoholics. *Journal of Studies on Alcohol* 38(7): 1247-1258.

El-Guebaly, N. and Offord, D.R. (1977) The Offspring of Alcoholics: A Critical Review. *American Journal of Psychiatry* 134(4): 357-65.

Ewing, J.A., Long, V., and Wenzel, G.G. (1961) Concurrent Group Psychotherapy of Alcoholic Patients and Their Wives.

International Journal of Group Psychotherapy **11**(3): 329-38.

Ewing, J.A. and Fox, R.E. (1968) Family Therapy of Alcoholism. In J. Masserman (ed.), *Current Psychiatric Therapies*. Vol. 8. New York: Grune and Stratton.

Fitch, M.J. (1975) Prospective Study in Child Abuse. Paper presented at the American Public Health Association Convention, Chicago, 1975. Cited in J. Mayer and R. Black (1977) The Relationship Between Alcoholism and Child Abuse and Neglect. In F.A. Seixas (ed.), *Currents in Alcoholism*. Vol. 2. *Psychiatric, Social and Epidemiological Studies*. New York: Grune and Stratton.

Fox, R. (1962) Children in the Alcoholic Family. In W.C. Bier (ed.), *Problems in Addiction: Alcoholism and Narcotics*. New York: Fordham University Press.

Gayford, J.J. (1975) Wife Battering: A Preliminary Survey of 100 Cases. *British Medical Journal* **1**: 194-197.

Gliedman, L.H., Rosenthal, D., Frank, J.D., and Nash, H.T. (1956) Group Therapy of Alcoholics with Concurrent Group Meetings with their Wives. *Quarterly Journal of Studies on Alcohol* **17**(4): 655-70.

Gomberg, E.S. (1974) Women and Alcoholism. In V. Franks and V. Burtle (eds), *Women in Therapy: New Psychotherapies for a Changing Society*. New York: Brunner/Mazel.

Gomberg, E.S. (1976) Alcoholism in Women. In B. Kissin and H. Begleiter (eds), *The Biology of Alcoholism*. Vol. 4. *Social Aspects of Alcoholism*. New York: Plenum Press.

Hill, R. and Hansen, D. (1962) The Family in Disaster. In G. Baker and D. Chapman (eds), *Man and Society in Disaster*. New York: Basic Books.

Hindman, M. (1975) Children of Alcoholic Parents. *Alcohol Health and Research World*. Winter 1975/1976: 2-6.

Hunter, G. (1963) Alcoholism and the Family Agency: With Particular Reference to Early Phase and Hidden Types. *Quarterly Journal of Studies on Alcohol* **24**(1): 61-79.

Jackson, D.D. (1957) The Question of Family Homeostasis. *Psychiatric Quarterly Supplement* **31**(1): 79-90.

Jackson, J.K. (1954) The Adjustment of the Family to the Crisis of Alcoholism. *Quarterly Journal of Studies on Alcohol* **15**: 562-88.

_____ (1962) Alcoholism and the Family. In D.J. Pittman and C.R. Synder (eds), *Society, Culture and Drinking Patterns*. New York: Wiley.

Jackson, J.K. and Kogan, K.L. (1963) The Search for Solutions: Help-Seeking Patterns of Families of Active and Inactive Alcoholics. *Quarterly Journal of Studies on Alcohol* 24(3): 449-72.

Jacob, T., Favorini, A., Meisel, S.S., and Anderson, C.M. (1978) The Alcoholic's Spouse, Children and Family Interaction. *Journal of Studies on Alcohol* 39(7): 1231-51.

James, J.E. and Goldman, M. (1971) Behavior Trends of Wives of Alcoholics. *Quarterly Journal of Studies on Alcohol* 32(2): 378-381.

Kammeier, M.L. (1971) Adolescents from Families with and Without Alcohol Problems. *Quarterly Journal of Studies on Alcohol* 32(2): 364-72.

Keane, A. and Roche, D. (1974) Developmental Disorders in the Children of Male Alcoholics. *Proceedings of the 20th International Institute on the Prevention and Treatment of Alcoholism*. Lausanne: International Council on Alcoholism and Addictions.

Lemert, E.M. (1960) The Occurrence and Sequence of Events in the adjustment of Families to Alcoholism. *Quarterly Journal of Studies on Alcohol* 21(4): 679-97.

Lindbeck, V.L. (1972) The Woman Alcoholic: A Review of the Literature. *International Journal of the Addictions* 7(3): 567-80.

Lisansky, E.S. (1957) Alcoholism in Women: Social and Psychological Concomitants: I. Social History Data. *Quarterly Journal of Studies on Alcohol* 18(4): 588-623.

Marsden, D. and Owens, D. (1975) The Jekyll and Hyde Marriages. *New Society*, May 8: 333-35.

Mayer, J. and Black, R. (1977) The Relationship Between Alcoholism and Child Abuse and Neglect. In F.A. Seixas (ed.), *Currents in Alcoholism*. Vol. 2. *Psychiatric, Social and Epidemiological Studies*. New York: Grune and Stratton.

McLachlan, J.F.C., Walderman, R.L., and Thomas, S. (1973) A Study of Teenagers with Alcoholic Parents. Toronto, Canada: Donwood Institute Research Monograph No. 3.

Meeks, D.E. and Kelly, C. (1970) Family Therapy with the

Families of Recovering Alcoholics. *Quarterly Journal of Studies on Alcohol* 31(2): 399-413.

Mik, G. (1970) Sons of Alcoholic Fathers. *British Journal of Addiction* 65(4): 305-315.

Moss, M.C. and Beresford Davies, E. (1967) *A Survey of Alcoholism in an English County*. Cambridge (Private Publisher).

National Institute on Alcohol Abuse and Alcoholism (1971) *Alcohol and Health: First Special Report to the Congress* (DHEW Publ. No. ADM-72-9099). Washington D.C.: US Government Printing Office.

Newell, N. (1950) Alcoholism and the 'Father Image'. *Quarterly Journal of Studies on Alcohol* 11(1): 92-6.

Orford, J., Guthrie, S., Nicholls, P., Oppenheimer, E., Egert, S., and Hensman, C. (1975) Self-Reported Coping Behavior of Wives of Alcoholics and its Association with Drinking Outcome. *Journal of Studies on Alcohol* 36(9): 1254-67.

Orford, J., Oppenheimer, E., Egert, S., Hensman, C., and Guthrie, S. (1976) The Cohesiveness of Alcoholism – Complicated Marriages and Its Influence on Treatment Outcome. *British Journal of Psychiatry* 128 (April): 318-39.

Paolino, T.J. and McCrady, B.S. (1977) *The Alcoholic Marriage: Alternative Perspectives*. New York: Grune and Stratton.

Parnitzke, K.H. and Prussing, O. (1966) Children of Alcoholic Parents. *Psychiatrie, Neurologie und Medizinische Psychologie* 18(1): 1-5. CAAAL Abstract No. 11524.

Renvoize, J. (1978) *Web of Violence: A Study of Family Violence*. London: Routledge and Kegan Paul.

Rosenbaum, B. (1958) Married Women Alcoholics at the Washingtonian Hospital. *Quarterly Journal of Studies on Alcohol* 19(1): 79-89.

Sclare, A.B. (1970) The Female Alcoholic. *British Journal of Addiction* 63(2): 99-107.

Scott, P.D. (1974) Battered Wives. *British Journal of Psychiatry* 125 (Nov.): 433-41.

Sloboda, S.B. (1974) The Children of Alcoholics: A Neglected Problem. *Hospital and Community Psychiatry* 25(4): 605-606.

Smith, C.J. (1969) Alcoholics: Their Treatment and Their

Wives. *British Journal of Psychiatry* **115**(526): 1039-1042.

Steele, B.F. and Pollock, C.A. (1968) A Psychiatric Study of Parents Who Abuse Infants and Small Children. In R. Helfer and H. Kempe (eds), *The Battered Child*. Chicago: University of Chicago Press.

Steinglass, P. (1977) Family Therapy in Alcoholism. In B. Kissin and H. Begleiter (eds), *The Biology of Alcoholism* Vol. 5. *Treatment and Rehabilitation of the Chronic Alcoholic*. New York: Plenum Press.

Steinglass, P., Weiner, S., and Mendelson, J.H. (1971) A Systems Approach to Alcoholism: A Model and its Clinical Application. *Archives of General Psychiatry* **24**(5): 401-408.

Stewart, W.R. (1970) Infant Neglect and Cruelty. *Proceedings of the 3rd International Conference on Alcoholism and Addictions*. Vol. 1: 215-22. Welsh Hospital Board.

Weir, W.R. (1970) Counseling Youth Whose Parents are Alcoholic: A Means to an End as Well as an End in Itself. *Journal of Alcohol Education* **16**(1): 13-19.

Wilson, C. and Orford, J. (1978) Children of Alcoholics: Report of a Preliminary Study and Comments on the Literature. *Journal of Studies on Alcohol* **39**(1): 121-42.

Young, L. (1964) *Wednesday's Children: A Study of Child Neglect and Abuse*. New York: McGraw-Hill.

6

MARGARET SHEEHAN
JACQUI WATSON

Members of the sub-group of the
Camberwell Council on Alcoholism
London

Response and recognition

This chapter is based on the work of a sub-group of the Camberwell Council on Alcoholism. This small group arose as a result of a growing interest in, and awareness of, an increasing number of women with alcohol problems. That there were, and are now, more women with alcohol problems is obvious. This increase is discussed elsewhere (chapter 1). The concerns of the sub-group of the Camberwell Council on Alcoholism were twofold. First, it looked at the services that were available for problem drinkers and their suitability for women. The second aim was to look at ways in which women with alcohol problems might be detected earlier in their drinking careers and so receive help sooner rather than later. Research on these topics in the UK is limited and, therefore, many of the ideas presented here are necessarily speculative. This chapter is, however, an attempt to draw together what information is available and to suggest possible ways of dealing with this problem.

The chapter will be divided into three sections:

  I. Current services that are available.
 II. Interaction of women and helping agents.
III. Recognition of alcohol problems in women.

I. Current services

In the United Kingdom there is a range of facilities on offer to problem drinkers, within the framework of the statutory and voluntary health and social services, as well as through private health facilities. This section will review the services available under the statutory and voluntary services and discuss their relevance to women problem drinkers. It will not consider those facilities in the private sector. They take clients only on a fee-paying basis and so eliminate quite a proportion of the population who may need help. They have their own network and are not widely advertized; there is a lack of readily-available information about them. The private sector largely offers out-patient treatment on a sessional basis with psychiatrists, psychotherapists, and hospital treatment in private clinics.

Services for problem drinkers in the United Kingdom suffer from a lack of co-ordination and integration. This was acknowledged in a Report by the Advisory Committee on Alcoholism to the Department of Health and Social Security (DHSS) and the Welsh Office. This Committee was set up to 'Advise ... on services relating to alcoholism and where appropriate to promote their development' (Advisory Committee on Alcoholism, 1978: ii). The report described the present arrangement of services as haphazard and patchy. There is a lack of co-ordination between the different social agencies, both statutory and voluntary, that are involved in helping problem drinkers.

The point of entry into the helping system is variable and many people working in the services do not know what help is available for people with alcohol problems. There is a widespread failure to appreciate the size of the problem, and an even greater ignorance about the growing numbers of women problem drinkers. There is also a failure to detect the problem in its early stages, when help would be most effective. In the following discussion, we describe those services that are seen and see themselves as having a direct role in providing help, and we exclude those services that may see a great many problem drinkers, but do not have an obvious role in their treatment, e.g. health visitors, prisons, hospital casualty departments. In general, we refer to services in England and Wales. Reference is made to Scotland where the information is available. The information presented is based on what was available at the time of writing, 1979.

(A) SPECIALIST STATUTORY SERVICES

(i) alcoholism treatment units

These are specialist units for the treatment of problem drinking within the National Health Service. They are usually attached to psychiatric hospitals. There are twenty-five in England and Wales, bur four of them do not take women. They provide a period of in-patient treatment using various methods. Nearly all use group psychotherapy and individual counselling after an initial period of detoxification. In addition, some provide occupational therapy, behavioural therapy, sensitivity training, and education about alcohol. In-patient units provide 537 beds. Some in-patient units take problem drinkers as day-patients. All provide out-patient counselling, and some provide out-patient therapy groups and social clubs. Admission to the in-patient units varies according to the individual unit's policy, e.g. one unit is non-selective and admits for a six-week programme of treatment only; another unit gives preference to treating all patients on an out-patient basis, and only admits those patients who have severe or more complicated problems. Some units will take crisis admissions, some cannot because of the pressures on beds. The majority of these units admit far fewer women than men. So, in cases where women do use the alcoholism treatment units, generally, they will find themselves in a minority. Their status as a minority is unavoidable because of the tendency in the units to do group work. Women problem drinkers in a larger group of problem drinkers face the additional disadvantage that the male members of the group frequently hold stigmatizing views about women who drink. In addition, it seems that women often have difficulties in discussing issues involving identity, sexual, and health problems in mixed sex groups.

(ii) detoxification centres

There are two of these, set up by the Department of Health and Social Security, to tackle the needs of habitual drunken offenders. The police may take to them intoxicated people whom they have apprehended, as an alternative to prosecution. The centres are short-stay and involve detoxifying the offender and motivating her or him towards rehabilitation. These centres are still at an experimental stage and are used almost entirely by men. One of these centres does not take women.

(B) SPECIALIST NON-STATUTORY SERVICES

These are social services provided by voluntary agencies which are funded partly from charitable sources and partly from grant aid from central and local government. Between them they cover a very similar range of services to those found in the statutory sector. There are no hospital services in this sector.

(i) counselling services

These are largely organized by local voluntary Councils on Alcoholism, of which there are twenty-three in England and Wales. There are also twenty-three in Scotland. In addition, other counselling services operate. These services aim to be easily accessible to the public and provide information, counselling, support, and referral, if necessary, on to other facilities. Some involve the families of problem drinkers in their approach and some also use group-work methods. It appears that this group of services sees a greater proportion of women than do others. For example, in 1978, the ratio of men to women attending fourteen counselling services run by Councils on Alcoholism was 2·5:1 (National Council on Alcoholism, 1978-79). These counselling services are usually located in premises that are designed to be easily accessible and non-stigmatizing – for instance, they are not attached to a hospital or council offices. They sometimes work on appointment systems which, in practice, tend to discourage those problem drinkers with more disorganized life-styles.

As already mentioned, these services are having some success in attracting a higher proportion of women clients. While the reasons for this are not yet obvious, it seems likely that the cause may be found in the ease of access to these services and their greater neutrality. Many of the services aim to provide easy access by having such features as premises in offices in high streets to which clients can walk in and sometimes can be seen without an appointment. There is also flexibility in opening hours. In addition, the staff of these agencies, who are very often volunteers, may be seen to have less statutory authority than other workers over their clients. This may be especially important to the woman who is afraid that her problem drinking may put her at risk of having her children taken away from her. It may also be the case that women prefer these centres because, on the whole, their contact is only with a counsellor.

(ii)   shop fronts

These centres are often based in highly accessible places like shopping centres, which have informal walk-in advisory services and they are usually designed to meet the needs of homeless problem drinkers. They provide advice, counselling, and support, and sometimes have direct access to other facilities such as hostels. From our experience, none of them have clear policies about attempting to meet the needs of women problem drinkers. Women tend to use them little, perhaps because of the tendency of homeless women problem drinkers to isolate themselves from Skid Row alcoholics.

(iii)   day centres

These provide advice, counselling, social support, and therapeutic activities on a basis of daily attendance at the centre. They aim to give more intensive support without the necessity of going into residential treatment. These centres report considerable variation in the extent to which they see women. Some aim at homeless problem drinkers and these see few women. Others aim at a broader treatment group and have had some success in attracting women clients. However, very few of these centres offer counselling to women clients. One day centre for problem drinkers reports that 34 per cent of their clients are women and that the proportion has increased annually since the centre started in 1976 (Accept Services UK, 1977). This latter example is a day centre with an explicit policy of endeavouring to meet the needs of women, a policy based on awareness of the increasing numbers of women problem drinkers and the failure of the services to respond to them. It is easily accessible by being a walk-in centre open seven days a week, and it provides a variety of responses to meet individual needs. It uses different treatment methods, including advice and counselling, group therapy, occupational therapy and assertion training, and, for women in particular, it provides the opportunity to use a woman's group and women counsellors if desired. It aims to help her familial needs not just by involving her family members in treatment, but also by alleviating child problems by permitting the mother to bring her child to the centre to be looked after there while she has treatment.

Some members of the sub-group of the Camberwell Council on Alcoholism (CCA) undertook a survey in 1978 (Litman and Wilson, 1978), to obtain a clearer picture of the facilities available to women with drink problems. The facilities surveyed were listed in the Directory of Projects (1976/77). This Directory gave details of statutory and non-statutory services for a variety of social problems. It included services for alcoholics. A sample was drawn of those facilities for alcoholics that stated that they provided services for female problem drinkers. The results of the non-residential facilities were interesting. Just under two thirds of the non-residential facilities were asked for information, and half of these replied. Although the results were from just under a third of the facilities, they did emphasize some important points. It is not intended to generalize from these results, but they do give an idea of the experience of particular projects. All the non-residential projects who replied reported that referrals of women problem drinkers were not as numerous as they would wish. The proportion of women whom these facilities saw ranged from 1 per cent to 50 per cent, and the average proportion was 35 per cent. When asked why they thought they had such low rates of referrals for women, the projects cited the following reasons: the hiddenness of female alcoholism, the reluctance of family members to expose a woman's drinking, stigma, the lack of awareness by public and referral agents, and the lack of the project's own resources to develop recognition policies.

These non-residential projects all reported difficulties in

referring women on to other agencies, and they gave the following reasons: lack of specialist accommodation for women, the lack of hostel places for single homeless women in many localities, the male orientation of the facilities, difficulties in organizing child care, and the reluctance of other agencies to receive the referral.

(iv) residential facilities

There are a range of facilities offering residential care for problem drinkers. They vary in the length of stay they offer (from a few weeks to a few years) and they vary in the amount of help they offer – from minimal practical support to intensive rehabilitation programmes. Most require the problem drinkers to abstain totally from alcohol and very few provide their own detoxification service. Most places are available in mixed-sexed hostels; there are two hostels which take women only.

In the CCA study of facilities (already referred to), the residential projects provided some useful information. Seventy per cent of the total number of beds listed in the Directory of Projects (above – iii) were represented. Just over half of the residential facilities replied to the request for information. The results are not intended to be seen as conclusive, but they do highlight some of the difficulties in this area. It did emerge that in some cases only 50 per cent of the beds available to women were being used by them (Litman and Wilson, 1978).

The reasons for the low take-up of vacancies in hostels has not been researched, but there are a number of suggested causative factors. Traditionally, the hostels, having been first set up for the homeless male alcoholic, have been dominated by male residents and this in itself may deter women applicants. The hostels are often seen as a last resort in treatment, both by applicants and by those who refer them there, and this may deter those women who resist identifying themselves with 'rock bottom' or Skid Row alcoholics. In addition, clinical experience supports the idea that many women retain their home-making skills longer than men. They are less likely to become homeless, and thus a hostel would need to be very attractive for them to want to relinquish their own home. Few of the hostels cater for people who want to retain their homes, and those that do have encountered financial difficulties in obtaining subsidies to come into the hostel while retaining their own home. A further resistance has been experienced among potential women applicants. Women who are struggling to hold their home and family together fear that by going into a hostel they expose themselves to the risk of their husbands divorcing them and to the risk of having their children taken into care.

(v)   Alcoholics Anonymous

This is a broad network of self-help groups organized entirely by recovering alcoholics, and placing great emphasis on confidentiality. It has more than 1,000 groups in England and Wales and most problem drinkers encounter Alcoholics Anonymous at some stage in their drinking career, despite Alcoholics Anonymous leaving it to the problem drinkers to approach them, rather than having a policy of actively encouraging people to come forward. It also has a parallel organization of self-help groups for the children and families of problem drinkers (Al-Ateen and Al-Anon). It has, at present, one group for women only. However, the ratio of women to men in the total organization is increasing – in 1964 it was 1:4·2; in 1976 it was 1:1·7 (Robinson, 1979). In most groups, women will be in a minority and find they cannot get sufficient support for the different ways in which their problem manifests itself.

(C)   NON-SPECIALIST STATUTORY SERVICES

(i)   General Practitioners in the National Health Service

General Practitioners are usually the first point of entry into the health service, and because of their broad contact with the general population on all matters of health, they see a great many problem drinkers. Some people who realize that they have a problem with drink will approach their GP for help first; many more do not, but take to their GP a problem that is related to their drinking. Some GPs are skilled at detecting drink problems and attempt either to deal with it themselves, or refer the patient on to a specialist facility, but there is evidence that the majority neither detect the problem nor know what to do with it when it presents itself (Shaw *et al.*, 1978).

(ii) social services departments of the local authorities

These have broad responsibilities for social work with the mentally ill, families and children, the elderly, and physically handicapped. While there is a tendency for many social workers to see problem drinking as a speciality outside their province, in practice, they see a great many problem drinkers. This is sometimes because problem drinkers approach them directly for help, but more often because they are involved with problems that are a consequence of problem drinking, e.g. family break-down. The problem drinking may often go undetected, but where it is detected there is often a reluctance to deal with the problem, and this reluctance appears to be more prevalent in the case of women problem drinkers.

Social services departments also have non-specialist day centres and hostels for the mentally ill, which sometimes admit problem drinkers. In practice these facilities often discourage problem drinkers because of the attitude that problem drinkers are more difficult to work with.

(iii) probation and after-care service

Many probation officers see problem drinkers because of behaviour that has brought them before the courts. The offence may be related to, or consequential on, their drinking. Less women are seen than men because of the lesser tendency of women to resort to crime and because the police are less likely to arrest women than men for drunkenness offences (see chapter 1).

(iv) other health care facilities

Some general hospitals will admit problem drinkers for detoxification. All see a great many problem drinkers when they are admitted for other health problems, some of which may be consequential on their drinking. They show a poor record for referral on to specialist agencies. Many problem drinkers are seen in Accident and Casualty departments of general hospitals following overdoses or road traffic accidents, but again there is a poor record for referral on.

Most psychiatric hospitals will admit problem drinkers to

their wards for treatment in non-specialized units, and many patients admitted for other disorders such as depression, and who then reveal a drink problem, are given help within the setting of general psychiatric units. The skill of any help given varies according to the training and attitudes of personnel. Some psychiatric hospitals have day hospitals where problem drinkers may go – units where patients may attend during the day to take advantage of more intensive support, but then return to their own homes at night, an arrangement that is designed to avoid some of the dangers of institutionalization. Most psychiatric units offer out-patient follow-up. Again, the extent to which these facilities are used by problem drinkers depends largely on the attitudes of the personnel running the facility.

(D) NON-SPECIALIST VOLUNTARY SERVICES

(i)   other agencies

Agencies such as the Samaritans, Family Welfare Association, the Marriage Guidance Council, and Citizens Advice Bureaux, frequently encounter problem drinkers among their clients. Again, the quality of help given varies according to the training and skills of the individual worker and their attitudes to problem drinking in women. There are a number of hostels for the mentally ill, and the homeless and rootless, which take care of problem drinkers. Eight of these are for women only.

We have referred to the varying capacity of these non-specialist groups of helping agents in both detecting and dealing with problem drinking in women. All these groups are subject to work overload, a factor that militates against their intervening effectively in new areas of work in which they will all have had only minimal training. For these groups it is easy to sidestep the problem by concentrating on the related or consequential problems, with which they know how to deal, and this tendency may be rationalized if the helping agent feels that problem drinking is hopeless to treat anyway. Alternatively, problem drinking may be seen as only a symptom of other problems which the helping agent may feel more confident about dealing with. In such cases, there may be a failure to give sufficient concern to the problem drinking itself, rationalized by a belief that the problem drinking will disappear if other fundamental problems are dealt with. A woman approaching the agent may find that she is not given sufficient help in acknowledging a problem that she is trying to hide anyway.

The reluctance of these agents to diagnose the problem in women may stem from an attitude that such a diagnosis can be so stigmatizing that it should be avoided for as long as possible. This is a recipe for disaster because it is only when the woman can acknowledge her problem that any help with it can be effective, and the earlier the help is received, the better the prognosis.

In the local authority social services it is known that many women are reluctant to admit to such a problem because of their fears that their ability to be capable as a mother will be questioned, and there may be a risk of having their children removed from them by statutory powers (although in practice this is very rarely the case). In addition, where the woman does have children, it is often the case that the children are given priority in the social worker's attentions because of the onerous social pressures on social workers to safeguard the wellbeing of the children referred to them.

In concluding this section, it should be pointed out that the majority of services for problem drinkers were set up at a time when female alcoholism was still a concealed problem, and inevitably the services were orientated towards the needs of men. The needs of women have not been seen to be different and there has been a failure to initiate new responses to meet those needs. In addition, stigmatizing attitudes that may be held by helping agencies are frequently not questioned and can have an extremely damaging effect. Many professional helping staff hold attitudes about the greater shamefulness of alcoholism in women; there is also a commonly held view that alcoholism is harder to treat in women than in men. This attitude may be unwittingly conveyed to the woman in treatment, thereby increasing her sense of despair and rendering her harder to treat. It is in the nature both of sexual stereotyping and the stigmatization process that most people will unconsciously collude with those processes while endeavouring to take a more rational position.

II.   Interaction of women and helping agents

This section is divided into two main parts. First, it looks at some of the ways women reach help with their alcohol problems. The second part deals with the problems helping agents may have in detecting and doing anything about alcohol problems. To illustrate our point we include some examples. These are based on clinical experience and do not relate to any specific person or persons.

(A)   INTERACTION OF WOMEN WITH AGENTS

In the first part of this section, we will look at women going to three different helping agents with a particular problem. The agents concerned were a General Practitioner, a medical officer at work, and a social worker. Following that, we will discuss the extremes that some women go to to get help and also their relief in being detected. Finally, we will give an example of where depression may also be present with an alcohol problem and that this need not make treatment impossible. The second part of this section will look at the confusion and lack of knowledge on the part of non-specialist workers in dealing with alcohol problems, and will look briefly at suggestions that have been made for improving the situation.

It is a fact that many women are in contact with a variety of helping agents, e.g. General Practitioners, health visitors, social workers, personnel managers, housing departments, lawyers, marriage guidance counsellors, etc. It is likely that they are presenting a different specific problem to each of these agencies or people, and it may be alcohol-related. They may go from agency to agency without the alcohol problem being picked up or, if it is, nothing is done about it. General Practitioners are one of the most likely groups that a woman might seek help from. The overt help sought might be for sleeplessness or depression, and it is possible that the GP will prescribe tranquillizers or sleeping tablets, and not discuss the effects of cross-tolerance between drugs and alcohol. One example:

A married woman had been a heavy drinker for most of her adult life. For many years she had worked as a barmaid and had drunk about six pints of stout a day while at work. She had never experienced drink as a problem until her late forties, when she lost two very close relatives, her father and son. As a result of this she became increasingly depressed and went to her GP. When he prescribed valium for her, she found it had little effect and that alcohol helped her much more to forget her grief. The more she drank, the easier it was for her to lose herself in an alcohol oblivion than to take some action to ameliorate her unhappy life situation. A year later she was drinking half a bottle of whisky a day, in addition to her customary six pints of stout. At this stage she went again to the GP, who this time referred her to an Alcoholism Treatment Unit.

A likely source of first contact for a working woman could be the medical officer at work. Even here, there is difficulty in picking up the alcohol problem, for example:

A middle-aged unmarried scientist was referred to a psychiatric hospital for treatment of depression by the medical officer of an international organization for which she worked. She had been in her job for many years. Only when she had been assessed at the hospital did it emerge that she had a longstanding problem with alcohol. She had, in fact, been alcohol dependent for about ten years at the time she was referred. For some years she had experienced alcohol withdrawal symptoms first thing in the morning, necessitating a drink before she went to work, and, during the course of the working day and the evening, she would consume about two bottles of whisky.

It is also apparent that some women with alcohol problems may have a lot of contact with an agency over a number of years, and yet the alcohol problem is not detected. Social workers are likely to have contact with certain clients over a long period for different social problems. Again, the alcohol problem often goes undetected, e.g.:

An unsupported mother, with a young family, who had drunk heavily for several years had shown symptoms of alcohol dependence for about two years. She had had intermittent contact with social workers for a few years. She had begun to worry about her drinking soon after experiencing withdrawal symptoms and, on the advice of a friend, went to an Alcoholics Anonymous meeting. She did not attend regularly as she found it hard to see herself as being like the other people in the Alcoholics Anonymous group who were mainly older men and had much more chronic drinking problems than hers. Her difficulties became obvious when she was caught shoplifting one day (beause she was short of money due to her drinking), and came to the attention of the courts. She was then referred by a probation officer to the out-patient department of an alcoholism treatment unit. Her drinking was not noticed to be problematic until she was caught shoplifting, and this was partly due to her drinking pattern.

One of the major problems with women's help-seeking in relation to alcohol problems is that they generally come for help as the result of a crisis or acute complication. In a study in Sweden (Dahlgren and Myrhed, 1977) of 100 alcoholics of each sex, it was found that women were admitted as a result of some emergency, e.g. a suicide attempt, and had to be forced into treatment by their families. This seems to be the pattern for many women who may have been showing signs of a problem for quite some time, but nothing has been done about it. Many women go to extremes to get help, e.g.:

A women who had been a heavy social drinker all her adult life did not experience problems with alcohol until she reached her mid-forties. Her marriage relationship deteriorated and her drinking increased. There were many rows and difficulties both with her husband and children. By this time she was experiencing a variety of withdrawal symptoms and needed to drink in the mornings to relieve them. Finally, she took an overdose. But in the casualty department to which she was taken following her overdose, no help was given for her problems. She returned home and took another overdose two months later. She was then referred to the out-patients department of an alcoholism treatment unit.

There are two main reasons suggested as to why it is difficult for women to come for help with their drinking problems. First, female problem drinking is much more likely to be secretive than male problem drinking. There are also more opportunities for a woman to drink in secret, e.g. they are frequently at home alone all day. Second, there is a much greater stigma attached to female problem drinking than there is to male problem drinking. There is tolerance, sometimes even active encouragement, for a man to drink too much. The fact that he is drunk is far more acceptable than if a woman were in the same position. Generally it can be said that there is social disapproval for people who become alcoholic. However, this disapproval is greater for women than for men. Loneliness and isolation are common to all problem drinkers, but to the woman, they are a greater problem. They will go to considerable lengths to conceal their drinking; they can also give the outward appearance of being controlled, and their children cared for. Also, if they are married, their husbands and families may want them to remain concealed. In the husband's case, if his wife is seen to have a drinking problem, it may be interpreted as a reflection on his masculinity.

Quite apart from the stigma attached to the woman drinking, there may be particular problems for different types of women. For example, a woman may fear that she will lose her children and husband if she is seen to have an alcohol problem and, as a result, is unable to cope. A working woman may be afraid of losing her job if her employer finds out, and the woman who is on her own, living at home, may be afraid of what the neighbours might think. All of these exacerbate the difficulty for the woman in asking for, and receiving help. In fact, for many, to be detected as having an alcohol problem may come as a great relief. An example:

> A woman in her early thirties was referred to the alcoholism counselling service in the out-patient department of a psychiatric hospital. She was living with her husband and five children in overcrowded accommodation on a run-down estate; her drinking had been causing problems for about two years prior to her referral. Her alcohol consumption had been putting strains on the limited family income, and her regular states of intoxication had been causing conflicts within the family, most obviously, in the relationship between herself and her husband.
>
> Her problem drinking appeared to date from the birth of

her last baby. The pregnancy and birth had been difficult. The youngest child turned out to be extremely active and demanding. At that time she had little support from her husband, who worked long hours and was unsympathetic to her problems of coping. She worked in a pub as a cleaner and brought home cans of lager to drink. Following a friend's advice she went to an Alcoholics Anonymous meeting. At this meeting she learned about some of the bad consequences of alcoholism, but she could not see herself ever being in that position. She was still perfectly well able to look after her children and home and also to go to her part-time job. However, the health visitor noticed that she had a problem with alcohol and referred her for treatment.

She was glad to see the alcoholism counsellor regularly. She still found it hard to accept the seriousness of her drinking, but she gained obvious relief from having a confidante, and, in addition, the counsellor was able to give her support on practical matters, like obtaining better housing and arranging for a day nursery for the youngest child.

As well as the alcohol problem, there may be a secondary diagnosis of depression. In a study in Sweden it was found in 'the woman treated for alcoholism, the diagnosis was in most cases combined with a psychiatric diagnosis, usually psychoneurosis or depressive reactions' (Dahlgren, 1978: 330). This added dimension of depression does not have to make treatment impossible, e.g.:

A single woman in her early fifties had drunk socially since her teens, but the pattern of her drinking had changed in her mid-forties and accelerated to about a bottle of brandy a day. Her GP referred her to the alcoholism department of a psychiatric hospital. He had known about the extent of her drinking for several years, but did not refer her on to a specialist facility until it seemed that she would lose her job because of the amount of time she missed work with 'hangovers'.

The alcoholism counsellor who saw her formed the impression that she was a deeply unhappy person. Her apathy, her retarded responses, her disturbed sleep and appetite were seen as typical of someone who was clinically depressed as they were of an alcohol dependent person. In counselling sessions, she talked about her life and several areas of distress emerged.

She attended counselling sessions for several months, and with the support she derived from the sessions, she was able to look at her difficulties and develop new ways of approaching them. She was able to withdraw from alcohol completely and responded well to treatment for her depression.

(B) DIFFICULTIES OF HELPING AGENTS

The difficulties for women with alcohol problems in being detected are compounded by the confusion and lack of knowledge on the part of non-specialist workers with whom they may come in contact. There is a reluctance on the part of many of these agents to take on this additional task. Also, many are unaware of the facilities that are available to help problem drinkers.

Many workers may feel that it is an invasion of privacy to ask a client about their drinking. This may be due to their own attitudes about the use and abuse of alcohol. If this is the case, how much harder it must be for workers to ask women about their drinking. It is likely, however, that these workers, e.g. GPs, social workers, health visitors, etc. will be the first point of contact for a woman with a drinking problem. In a general population survey in 1974 (Shaw *et al.*, 1978: 123)

> 'it transpired that, on average, these respondents who reported the heaviest consumption (of alcohol) and the most problems from drinking, had a rate of contact with professional helpers, three times higher than the rest of the sample and yet, as far as could be detected, none of them had received any help specifically for their drinking problems.'

Much of the reluctance of these workers may be due to a lack of knowledge on the topic and a feeling that it is not their responsibility to tackle this area, allied with a feeling of hopelessness in responding to people with an alcohol problem. This hopelessness may be the result of many workers feeling that they are untrained to help and that there is little that can be achieved with this problem. It may be that some have tried in the past, failed, and then given up. They may give up because of the pressure of their own jobs and the fear that to tackle the alcohol problem will be too great. An example:

An elderly widow living in a run-down area found it impossible to manage on her state pension and, having got into arrears with her rent, went one day to her local social services office to ask for help. It was clear to the social worker on that first occasion that she had a problem with drink: when seen she smelt strongly of alcohol, her gait was unsteady, and her speech was slow and sometimes slurred. On that first occasion she would not admit that drink played a part in her inability to manage her financial affairs, but as she came to know the social worker, she became more open. The social worker saw her regularly and encouraged her to use a local day centre, and helped her with rent arrears. She cut back on her drinking for a time, but then relapsed again. At this time, the social worker herself was very pressured and she was not aware of the facilities for problem drinkers and, having deployed the resources she did have at her disposal, she thought there was nothing more to be done.

The lack of knowledge about alcohol and the reluctance to ask questions about it is borne out by a study of general community agents. This revealed 'that less than 10 per cent of community agents [GPs, social workers, and probation officers] had received any education or training whatsoever in dealing with alcohol abuse and that the training of the "educated agents" had generally been limited to less than one day' (Shaw *et al.*, 1978: 130). In this study it was found that the agents in most cases did not detect the drinking problem themselves. They had been informed of it by someone else. The main reason for this lack of detection was that they were unaware of the indicators of such a problem. Although the problems that are often associated with alcohol abuse continue – neglect of children, gastritis, etc. – the actual possibility of an alcohol problem is not explored.

It appeared from this study that it was not enough just to give non-specialist workers information about alcohol. To be supported in their new role was a very important part of acquiring this new knowledge. The lack of support for the non-specialists is of crucial importance. The study states that, 'general community agents did not feel supported by the existing specialist services' (Shaw *et al.*, 1978: 140). The non-specialist services were also ambivalent about the effectiveness and competence of the specialist services.

The feelings of the non-specialist workers – lack of skills, unsure of their responsibilities, and lacking support – have important implications for the specialist services. Within the alcohol field generally, there has been a move away from in-patient treatment, except where necessary, to more out-patient, community-based facilities. There has been an increase in the number of walk-in counselling facilities. It has been argued that non-specialist workers can deal with alcohol problems. 'Professional workers with basic skills, such as general practitioners and generic social workers, are to be asked to play a large part in the treatment and care of people with alcohol problems' (Advisory Committee on Alcoholism, 1978: 3). These workers are referred to as primary workers. In addition to these there are probation officers, health visitors, Samaritans, Citizens Advice Bureaux, marriage guidance counsellors and personnel officers. These, and others, may be the primary point at which a woman with a drinking problem makes contact. The Advisory Committee's Report continues,

'the knowledge and skill required at the primary level lie, we believe, properly within the compass of generally trained professional staff . . . the knowledge and skill required is relatively simple and is appropriate to non-specialist professional staff . . . For many, this will require a change in attitudes as well as the gaining of the requisite knowledge and skills.' (Advisory Committee on Alcoholism, 1978: 3)

This also implies the need for more co-operation between different workers, agencies, both specialists and non-specialists.

Some success has been reported about attempts to increase knowledge about the needs of women with alcohol problems. The interested group of people who were the initiators of this book and, in particular, this chapter, responded to specific requests for such help. A programme was developed to help health visitors to detect alcohol problems more easily and to refer on appropriately. Another attempt was to help devise a facility for female problem drinkers who were living in an American Air

Force base in Britain. This again focused on the particular needs of women and suggested the most appropriate forms of treatment. These are only small beginnings, but they do illustrate what can be done if necessary and without an enormous extra workload. Much of the efforts would be greatly enhanced if local information regarding facilities was readily available and disseminated. Ideally, one would hope that,

> 'within each community there should be a team, however loosely defined . . . Every community has problem drinkers, although the number may not be known precisely. The sorts of problems vary in extent from place to place. Consequently, the facilities needed will also vary. Those concerned with problem drinkers must contact others with a similar interest within their community and build up as many links as possible. This will enable each one to become aware of the various forms of help readily available.' (Advisory Committee on Alcoholism, 1978: 3)

III.   Recognition of alcohol problems in women

We have looked at the difficulties in women being detected at an early stage with their alcohol problems. These were due to two main reasons. The first was the secretiveness of female drinking and the stigma associated with it. The second reason was the reluctance of workers to ask questions about alcohol use and also the ignorance about existing facilities. These two reasons interact to create a situation of anxiety and generate feelings of helplessness and hopelessness, both for the women and workers. In this section, we attempt to look at some of the indicators of drinking problems in women and so, it is hoped, to encourage detection at an earlier stage.

The first part of this section will describe the areas of a woman's life that might indicate stress in relation to alcohol – personal relationships, physical appearance, financial difficulties, and legal problems. The second section will discuss in general terms the kinds of women who may be susceptible to alcohol problems. In concluding the chapter we will suggest certain features that need to be taken into account in the treatment of women with alcohol problems.

(A) INDICATORS

Alcohol, as a drug that affects mood, will inevitably have a marked effect on personal interactions. At the level of social drinking, the effect may be frequently beneficial, enabling the woman to be more relaxed with those around her. But the woman who is drinking heavily may be subject to more pronounced mood changes, and there may be a frequency of occasions when she is 'out of step' with those around her. The lowering of inhibition that accompanies intoxication may produce behaviour that at best may be mildly incomprehensible and even amusing, but at worst may be actively anti-social, with the drinker becoming angry and abusive, or even violent. A woman who becomes incapable of functioning normally because she is intoxicated will need increased support from the friends around her, and, as they begin to question the recurrence of such states, it may become necessary for the woman problem drinker to defend her precarious position by evasion or deceit. Such behaviour may eventually lead to the alienation of those close to her and the breakdown of those relationships. In addition, it may become increasingly difficult to initiate new personal relationships as her life becomes increasingly dominated by the need for alcohol. At such a stage, men problem drinkers tend to seek out other problem drinkers, but, as already described, women are more likely to drink alone, probably because of the guilt they feel about their behaviour. For them to seek out other problem drinkers will require them to make an identification that they are trying to resist.

Drunken women are frequently viewed as more promiscuous than drunken men. While there is no evidence that this is actually the case, it seems highly probable that the lowering of sexual inhibitions that occurs during intoxicated states will incur greater disapproval when it occurs in women than when it occurs in men, because of the different standards of sexual morality that apply to men and women. Societal disapproval of women who have multiple sexual relationships may be viewed as an attempt to protect the nuclear family; similarly, all problem drinking may be seen as a threat to the family because it directly interferes with the woman's capacity to perform her role as wife and mother, and it follows that where problem drinking occurs within a marriage, severe strains will be put on the marital relationship, and there will be a high risk of breakdown. It will also add an extra dimension of tension in her relationship with her children. The children may manifest the strain in a variety of ways. Some of the more common ones are behavioural difficulties in school, truanting, acting-out behaviour like theft, running away, or maybe even drinking themselves. Many such children report feeling anxious and lacking in confidence.

Along with the breakdown of personal relationships will undoubtedly go a deterioration in personal appearance. The drinking may be apparent in symptoms such as confusion, incoherence, poor co-ordination, and even obvious intoxication, as well as the smell of alcohol on the breath.

As problem drinking increases, there will be financial problems as the woman spends an increasing proportion of her resources on alcohol, and there will be practical problems as she becomes increasingly less able to cope with daily tasks, either because she is inebriated or because she is suffering from the withdrawal effects of alcohol. At home there may be a decline in personal standards of housework, and there may be arrears in the rent or mortgage – which may eventually lead to her eviction. Budgetting and meeting financial commitments may become increasingly problematic – unless the person is on a high income. Employment difficulties are commonplace. In the beginning, the problem drinker may become increasingly unpunctual or need to take frequent sick leave because of the effects of hangovers and withdrawal symptoms. As dependence progresses, she may need to drink during the course of the working day to stave off further withdrawal symptoms and cravings. Once this is discovered (and this may not be for some time if the person works in an unsupervised setting), the employer may dismiss her. Her condition may eventually render her incapable of doing her job and, if the situation continues, there will be dismissal, a pattern that will repeat itself in the next job if the problem is not dealt with.

Legal problems may also be indicators of problem drinking and may bring the woman in contact with the courts. The breakdown in family relationships may lead to separation or divorce proceedings, as well as struggles between parents for custody of the children. Financial difficulties may lead to the woman being taken to court for debt. She may come into contact with the criminal courts for offences such as drunken driving, being drunk and disorderly, or theft (the latter often because it has been necessary to steal to obtain money for drink). Sometimes these offences are of an irrational nature. They may be committed while the woman is drunk and show no obvious motive beyond that of her seeking attention for her desperate plight.

(B) GENERAL DISCUSSION

Breakdown in family relationships, financial, legal, and housing problems are not peculiar to women problem drinkers. Neither are the problems of isolation and loneliness. Nor can it be said that these are solely the result of problem drinking. Many people in our society suffer from these problems and there are many women who have to live with these difficulties. It is fair to say, however, that any woman having these difficulties may recourse to alcohol as a way of coping. There are no particular groups of women who alone are susceptible to these difficulties. It is important to emphasize that there may be some women who are more at risk than others, and are more vulnerable to problems at different periods in their lives. When this is so, it is essential to recognize that there may be an alcohol component in the problems. It may appear to be a beneficial way of coping with these problems. Particular groups of women who may be at risk are unsupported or separated mothers, particularly those with young children, women who are at home all day or women whose families are leaving home. The woman who has lived most of her life looking after elderly parents and then in her later years finds herself alone, has now to find a whole new way of life. The working woman who has to compete with men to prove she can do the job as well as they can may also 'drink like a man' to be accepted. Lesbians are another group of women who may be vulnerable because of the social unacceptability of their position in our society.

From a physiological point of view, some problem drinkers are known to use alcohol to cope with physical distress. This applies equally to men and women. For women, there are a number of conditions associated with their sexual identity that may be associated with problem drinking, e.g. abortion, post-partum depression, hysterectomy, and the menopause. These events can be very traumatic for a woman, both in terms of the upheaval to her life and the threat to her identity as a woman.

All of this points to the need to be aware of the fact that different kinds of women at different stages in their lives may use alcohol to cope with their problems, and also the multi-faced nature of an alcohol problem. There may be one event that triggers the onset of uncontrolled drinking, but if one looks at the case history of a woman with a drinking problem, it will become obvious that there are a number of clues as to the reasons for her drinking. Gomberg (1976) in her review of the American literature on the woman alcoholic says, 'physiological predisposing factors, plus the psychological predisposing factors and social predisposing factors add up to a high potential for alcoholism'. It is the combination of these factors that may trigger problem drinking.

(C) CONCLUSION

In conclusion, this chapter gives an overview of what are considered to be important factors in the treatment of women with alcohol problems. It is very important that there is a greater individualization of response to women. This implies a flexibility of treatment in gearing it towards the specific needs of each woman.

It is still essential to look at the alcohol problem first, but the other problems should not be ignored, e.g. marital, social, and occupational difficulties. It is worth considering including the important people in her life in her treatment, e.g. husband, family, boyfriend, etc. The necessity for long-term support and follow-up cannot be underestimated. If treatment is to be effective there will be changes in the woman. The other people in her life may find it difficult to adjust to these changes just as much as the woman may have difficulty in maintaining them.

On a practical level, it may be that if a woman has young children and is attending a day centre, nursery facilities may need to be provided. In utilizing existing services or in planning new ones, account must be taken of appropriate opening times for particular women, e.g. women who work will not be able to go during the day, whereas women with school-going children might more readily use day-time facilities. The place where treatment is undertaken, be it a walk-in counselling point or a hospital out-patients department, needs to be welcoming and encouraging. Also, it should offer the security of acceptance and confidentiality. The services and facilities that are available need to be advertized in a sensitive and imaginative way, so as to reach women appropriately.

The adequate education and training of workers who deal with female problem drinkers cannot be over-emphasized. Inherent in this is the need to examine the attitudes and assumptions of workers about alcohol use and abuse in general, and how these attitudes relate to women in particular. Cognisance needs to be taken of the role and recognition given to woman's position in our society. Many of the stereotypical attitudes about women will, it is hoped, change as the status of women improves and their particular needs are recognized and met.

References

Accept Services UK (1977) *2nd Annual Report*: 27.

Advisory Committee on Alcoholism (1978) *The Pattern and Range of Services for Problem Drinkers*. Report to the Department of Health and Social Security and Welsh Office: ii-25.

Dahlgren, L. (1978) Female Alcoholics. III Development and pattern of problem drinking. *Acta Psychiatrica Scandinavia* **57**: 325-35.

Dahlgren, L. and Myrhed, M. (1977) Female Alcoholics: Ways of Admission of Alcoholic Patients. A study with special reference to the alcoholic female. *Acta Psychiatrica Scandinavia* **56**: 39-49.

Gomberg, E.S. (1976) The Female Alcoholic. In R.E. Tarter and A.A. Sugerman (eds), *Alcoholism: Interdisciplinary Approaches to an Enduring Problem*: 608. Reading, Mass: Addison Wesley Publishing Co. Inc.

Litman, G.K. and Wilson, C. (1978) A Review of Services for Women Alcoholics in the U.K. Paper presented at the 24th International Institute on the Prevention and Treatment of Alcoholism, Zurich.

National Council on Alcoholism (1979) *2nd Annual Report 1978-1979*: 38.
Robinson, D. (1979) *Talking out of Alcoholism: The Self-Help Process of Alcoholics Anonymous*. London: Croom Helm.
Shaw, S., Cartwright, A., Spratley, T., and Harwin, J. (1978) *Responding to Drinking Problems*. London: Croom Helm.

7

ANNABEL PAGE

Social Worker
Scalebor Park Hospital
West Yorkshire

Counselling

Because there is so much confused thinking about the problem of women drinkers it is hardly surprising that what is on offer in terms of treatment is tremendously variable. This is not, it would seem, because of recognized reluctance to take on a more 'difficult' group with a poorer prognosis.

There is a scarcity of information on what helps women drinkers and what information there is often leads to contradictory conclusions (Birchmore and Walderman, 1975). However it is clear that women do underuse facilities open to both men and women, (Litman and Wilson, 1978) and that though, as research indicates, female alcoholics do differ from male alcoholics, these differences are not reflected in treatment programmes. It may be that women find it difficult to seek and accept help and that domestic situations limit the suitability of many facilities but it also remains true that these facilities, programmes, and methods of treatment were originally designed with male alcoholics in mind and are not necessarily effective in treating female alcoholics. Certainly though, the flaws may not be in the methods themselves but rather in an inflexible and ill-considered blanket application, arising from the assumption that alcoholism is a disease wherein sex is irrelevant. Now that increasing numbers of women are coming forward for help, some efforts are being made to provide 'extras' for them, but such provision occurs within regimes that are still male oriented. There is no real questioning of what needs to be provided for women, what plans need to be thought out, campaigned for, and put into practise, given the continuing and rapid rise in the rates of problem drinking amongst women. There may be some reluctance to do this, not only because it means challenging traditionally and well-accepted assumptions and methods, but also because it may mean providing new resources involving staff, time, and money.

This chapter will examine the major treatment methods in use for alcoholics generally, then discuss whether these are, or are not, the best ways to help women drinkers. Particular attention will be paid to the application of treatment methods and to the attitudes of counsellors, for it may be that it is a question of adapting existing methods and resources to provide suitable help. The chapter will, of course, concentrate on treatment methods based on counselling rather than on medical treatment, which is not within the scope of the author. However it must be stressed that every counsellor and social worker must have a thorough working knowledge of the symptoms and medical problems likely to be found in drinkers, and recognize the importance of obtaining a thorough medical assessment so that the attention so often needed will be given.

Counselling

If we take a general definition of counselling – 'helping through caring, listening, prompting, with a clarification of motives' (Halmos, 1978: 2 and 3) we have a broad enough view to avoid the need for distinction between psychotherapy, casework, and other similar forms of treatment. All counselling procedures share a method, in being 'talking cures' which attempt treatment through clarification of subjective experiences and meaning, with some element of advice-giving according to the context and one's therapeutic role. On the question of what special qualities are needed for the counsellor facing the individual alcoholic, and the woman alcoholic in particular, it is impossible to prescribe definitively. It is generally thought that alcoholics do not need a different approach; they and their families are human beings in trouble, but it is perhaps particularly important with this group to be 'honest, loving and informed' (Spratley, 1974:

7); to be reliable and flexible, and to concentrate on establishing an open positive relationship from the beginning. As Spratley (1974) points out, having established a good working relationship, the counsellor and client must together try to understand the role that alcohol has played in the client's life for better and for worse. The counsellor needs to understand the clients' notions of the beneficial effects alcohol has had for them, while the clients need to understand the harmful effects, as these will be crucial factors in motivating them to change their behaviour. It is difficult for the counsellor to persist in helping the client who continues to drink in a harmful manner unless s/he deeply understands the seemingly good effects that the client obtains from drinking. And women do see their drinking as having beneficial effects. Some report their drinking as escapist, with alcohol acting as an anaesthetic whereby they can forget worries and relieve tension or nervousness. Others say they drink to relieve feelings of loneliness and inferiority or to feel more acceptable socially or because they could not adequately fulfil a satisfying role within the family unit.

Characteristics of women alcoholics relevant to counselling

First, it must be remembered that women alcoholics are a heterogeneous group with some recognizable subgroups, differentiated on the basis of social class and pattern of upbringing, drinking practices, and so forth (Beckman, 1975). However what is clear is that women show a different pattern of 'illness' and different characteristics from those of male alcoholics. It is these differences that are important and they should be guides to what help women need, given the individuality and life setting of each person.

   Perhaps the most important factor is how an alcoholic woman views herself and the change she needs to make in her self-image. This will involve her looking at her total life experience from childhood, her current situation, the effect of society's view on her, and, crucial to treatment, the attitude of the treatment agencies and helpers involved with her. There are indications that many women drinkers have experienced severe deprivation, such as loss of a parent through divorce, desertion, or death in early life and have often suffered other emotional traumas.

Women alcoholics are more likely to have had alcoholic parents and alcoholic siblings, and in adult life have a high rate of marital instability, psychiatric problems, and suicide attempts.

One study suggests that women problem drinkers are 'self-defeating, vulnerable, pessimistic, withdrawn and sensitive to criticism' (Beckman, 1975: 807). It is generally accepted that these women suffer from low self-esteem and that until this view of themselves as personally inadequate is altered they will not be able to enter into treatment in a constructive way.

It is likely that this low self-esteem and poor self image is a result not only of women drinkers' general psychological development but also of society's view of their drinking as shameful and degrading. Counsellors must be clearly aware of both their own and the general public's attitude to women drinkers and their prognosis:

'As a rule women alcoholics are not seen in clinics or hospitals until the drinking problem has gone on for some years. It is likely that the social consequences of the drinking problem i.e. family break up, job dismissal, rejection by friends and associates, and general social disapproval are greater for the woman alcoholic who is known as such. The woman patient who appears at a clinic or hospital after years of uncontrolled drinking could therefore conceivably be a more disturbed individual than her male counterpart as a result of her alcoholism and its socially punishing consequences, and not because she was initially, in her pre-alcoholic personality, a more disturbed individual.' (Lisansky, 1957: 596)

It is only realistic to see that women drinkers, because of these interwoven strands of experience in their lives, will present counsellors with particular difficulties and challenges. They do tend to deny their problems and resist therapeutic intervention even more than male drinkers, but this denial and hopelessness should become the centre of therapeutic intention rather than the cause of labelling women alcoholics as having from the start a poor prognosis. We will only add to these women's unsatisfactory life experiences and only reinforce their poor self-image if we have no faith in ourselves to help and none in them to be helped. Anxieties, doubts, and difficulties should be aired and worked on in counsellors' supervision sessions since 'the optimism or pessimism of the therapist can play a subtle and significant part in the outcome [of treatment]' (Gomberg, 1976: 157).

Another characteristic of many women problem drinkers is that they frequently link their excessive drinking to psychological stress and a specific unhappy experience. This crisis, which is often a loss or breakdown of a significant relationship, may well be felt as a life blow because of its emotional connection with the person's disrupted relationships in early life. It is often the case that a woman facing the loss of her husband or children may feel that she loses her identity with them. These particular experiences are felt to be intolerable and the individual does not find the resources internally or externally to adjust to and work through the crisis. Alcohol is found to provide relief, whether or not the woman drank much prior to the crisis, and it is a common picture to find drinking, and consequently symptoms, telescoped in these women.

It is important, too, to bear in mind the link between depression and drinking for women; the drinking may be secondary to and masking an underlying psychiatric disorder. Many women use other drugs as well as alcohol to help them cope with difficulties and may suffer joint dependence. There have also been links made between alcoholism in women and their physiological functioning, though there seems no clear evidence that drinking is directly related to premenstrual tension among alcoholic women. Perhaps what is most helpful to counsellors is to learn from these theories the importance to women's overall emotional adjustment of accepting feminine physiological functions, and helping their clients to do so.

Finally, mention must be made again of the need for counsellors to be in touch with, and sensitive to, changing social ideas which have such a strong bearing on the increase of drinking amongst women. Sex-role conflicts must be taken into account when working with alcoholic women on their adjustment to life without the need to drink. This is such a complex and current issue that we must always as counsellors be alive to our own 'state of play' and be clear what belongs to us and what belongs to our clients. If not we may be in danger of pushing some women drinkers along the traditional, or emancipated, pathway for our own ends and beliefs rather than theirs.

Groups

Working with alcoholics in groups has been the traditional method of treatment for what was originally an almost entirely male clientele. There has been no clear evidence to demonstrate that this method of help is as appropriate to women as to men and many practitioners have expressed doubts as to its efficacy for women, as a result of their own observations and of comments made by women consumers.

Let us first examine what group-work for alcoholics means and the various groups likely to be used.

Belonging to a group satisfies very basic human needs; it provides a sense of companionship, a relief of aloneness, and a safe place where one can express oneself and be accepted and cared about; where one can be heard and can listen to and respond to others. The group itself develops meaning, strength, and value, different from the sum of the individual relationships between group members. If it goes no further we can see how such a group will be a tremendous help to those alcoholics whose sense of identity and worth has been undermined by their drinking and who are likely to feel cut off from others and sure that no one can understand or share their pain, frustration, and sense of helplessness. For some, that acceptance and freedom to 'be real' will be enough to lift them to a level where they can then use their own resources to understand and help themselves. They are the lucky ones likely to have so called 'intact personalities', good family support, and whose lives, morale, and relationships have not become distorted through years of drinking.

For most, their situations and abilities to understand, face, and believe in themselves without the need for alcohol will be a longer, more painful process, but a group can provide a framework of relationships where this work can be done over time. Members can explore, reveal, and learn different aspects of themselves and how others see them. Their intrapsychic conflicts may be revealed by inconsistencies in behaviour and expression of feelings and their confused relationships demonstrated by what they project onto, and receive from other group members. It is a place where they can test reality and themselves as they slowly learn who they are without alcohol, and what others really feel about them. Much of this will be painful, if it means learning to accept qualities and feelings they do not like, and distressing if it involves re-experiencing painful events and relationships. But if the group remains committed to caring, acceptance, honesty, and work, members can be 'held' through the most painful times and become stronger and more secure. What is perhaps the most therapeutic aspect of these groups is that the 'treatment' is done by and received by all. For those who may well have been feeling worthless, dishonest, resentful, and powerless at least at some level inside themselves, the awareness that they are the stuff of this treatment, that they can give and be given to, and make something work, is a new satisfaction.

It is the group leader's job to work out a contract with the group, (reasons for being there; time commitment; any basic rules and structure), to exploit the interactions within the group, to keep them to their task, to keep boundaries, to be clear, honest, and involved, but never to detract from the ultimate gain members will get from doing their own work. It is important to be clear about tasks, aims, and membership and it is perhaps in this area that the debate about whether or not women are helped by groups should be focused.

It would seem puzzling and sad if women were not able to share in the gains of the group as described. Yet Curlee (1968: 19) is often quoted for her observation that 'women alcoholics seem to find it difficult to become part of a group except on a very superficial level, or to find a meaningful comradeship and warmth that helps men so much'. She also observes that women are sometimes able to relate well to comparatively few people within the group, but that the real feeling of membership and group participation often seems to be missing. Curlee thinks that this may be due in part to male group members' attitudes, but she also suggests that group membership just does not have the same meaning for women as for men. Perhaps this may be linked to their previous drinking habits: men being more accustomed to drinking in groups, and women to drinking in solitude.

In another study (Mayer and Green, 1967) of group work with female alcoholic ex-offenders (perhaps a rather specialized group), it was found that group members related individually with the leader, rather than with one another, were preoccupied with feelings of rivalry, and did not reach a stage of group cohesion.

The main groups likely to be operating for alcoholics are as follows: mixed-sex groups – whether in- or outpatient or Alcoholics Anonymous groups; single-sex groups mainly for women only; and 'couple' groups. Some of the groups will have a clear therapeutic label and be (or should be) clear about their tasks, about membership, and about time length. These groups will probably be run according to the style, training, and orientation of the leader(s). Certain techniques such as role play, relaxation exercises, and psychodrama may be used to encourage experimentation with new behaviours and expressions. These techniques will be of particular help to women drinkers who may need to learn new social skills, to find ways of handling anxiety and nervousness without drink, and to develop their capacity to be assertive. Some group meetings may be given over to discussions on set topics, films, talks, and have a clearly educational aim, but group interaction can still be observed and made use of in quite structural settings.

Alcoholics Anonymous, Al-Anon, and Al-Ateen offer the widest network of support for recovering alcoholics and their families. Their groups are ostensibly leaderless (though strong personalities may dominate them), likely to be mixed-sex groups, and without a time limit for members. A social survey of Alcoholics Anonymous in England and Wales was carried out in 1977 comparing affiliation and attendance then with samples – in 1964 and 1972. Results show that women have joined Alcoholics Anonymous in growing numbers. However, it is failing to attract young people of either sex with drinking problems (Robinson and Henry, 1977).

Women-only groups have been set up in a variety of settings, generally as a response to the increase in women drinkers and as a recognition of their differences. The push for them is likely to have come from those particularly interested in and concerned over treatment issues for these women.

We know that what drives women drinkers to seek help are family and interpersonal difficulties rather than troubles at work, as is the case with men (Sclare, 1975). This and the other mutual concerns of women alcoholics would indicate that such groups are vital. Indeed if raising low self-esteem and working on identity problems are such crucial areas with women drinkers, women-only groups should be a focus, rather than purely an adjunct to mixed-sex groups, at least during the initial stages of treatment.

It was noted at Scalebor Park Alcoholic Unit, an inpatient mixed-sex unit, that newly-admitted women, do behave differently in a woman-only group. In the daily mixed-sex group (where they were outnumbered 3 to 1) they remained quiet or chatted and flirted mildly and awkwardly while the men moved in on serious subjects related to their drinking and why they were in the unit. The women remained at a level of looking to the staff members for support, encouragement, and permission to speak while the men began to talk more freely between themselves. When the women attended the weekly women-only group they lost their awkwardness and apparent 'silliness' and soon looked to each other and got down to the business of why they were there. They were still somewhat inclined to look to the staff members for permission and approval but far less so than in the mixed group. One factor in this difference may have been that the group was smaller, but it is also possible that their customary roles and ways of behaving inhibited them. Another observation is that women are often less experienced in being in groups other than 'chat' groups with other women. Men mix in groups in a variety of ways, generally centred round work, and may be more used to speaking up for themselves. In other words men have learned the habit of interacting in groups with a sense of their own authority, in a way that many women have yet to learn. It follows from this that women would benefit from being in an all-women group partly to 'catch up' on this skill as well as to share common concerns, before moving into a mixed sex group. It will be likely that women in such a group will need to express a good deal of guilt, rage, and disappointment, and need encouragement and help to do so, but it would be unhelpful if the theme of such groups became a repetitive complaint about men. In one such group it became the group norm to have 'bad' husbands/lovers and there was pressure on new members to conform to this view. 'Surely you drank because you have had bad experiences with men?' was asked of a newcomer who was being well supported by a concerned husband. Leaders need to help groups question such fixed norms, and look more deeply at the rage and underlying fear of change. The anger is often as much to do with their view of themselves, or that originally felt towards or modelled on their rejecting mothers, as it is to do with their husbands. They need to be helped to locate and understand the anger, and use it constructively. There are many issues to fight for, once these women can accept and value themselves.

This stress on women-only groups is to give them their right place and value, not to underrate the importance of the experience for women as well as men of being in a mixed-sex group. After a preparatory period in individual counselling or in a women-only group they may then move on to a mixed-sex group. Only in a mixed-sex group will a woman be able to explore fully how she sees men then test out and learn new and more satisfying and flexible ways of relating to them, and to correct her stereotypes. It should be an opportunity, unlike any other, to know men and be equal, rather than being a submissive or rebellious daughter, lover, or wife. Such learning will be enhanced if co-therapists of both sexes work with these groups. They can act as models, correct projections, and help each other recognize and deal with any of their own unconscious biases.

There has been some work reported on 'multiple-couple' group therapy approaches to alcoholism and concurrent groups for alcoholics and spouses. It is a sad fact that wives of alcoholics are more likely to participate than husbands of female alcoholics. These groups may be run using group techniques (Steinglass, 1977) or family therapy principles, and results are encouraging in that they link improvement in the marriage with reduction of drinking. The significance (in terms of its link to prognosis) of involving spouses, will be discussed in the next section when looking at working with the family. Certainly if a 'multiple-couple' approach is helpful to alcoholics, men and women, then such groups shall play a more crucial role in treatment. We might hypothesize that, apart from a simple lack of desire to move away from the known and comfortable group settings with the identified patient alone, such groups might well raise the anxiety level of workers. Our fantasies of four or five sets of quarrelling couples proving too difficult for us to control and cope with, may be leading to an avoidance of experimenting with a way of working that might not only be therapeutically valuable to our clients and their partners, but enlightening for us.

If we accept the initial statement made regarding the ordinary but significant satisfactions and rewards gained from belonging to and working in groups, we need to help and encourage women to learn to participate rather than allow ourselves to say too easily that groups are not for them at any stage. Indeed, since women need to be helped to find more resources for themselves in their world and find areas where they can get positive feedback and peer group validation, affiliation to groups in the community will be of great benefit. For some who are challenging their traditional wife/mother role and seeking to broaden their identity, affiliation to women's movement groups may be the place to work at this. Having an occupation outside the home, joining community action groups, pressing for local resources that have a meaning to them, joining mutual-interest groups, developing new talents, and learning new skills at classes – all these can be rewarding, enriching experiences. Women drinkers who have worked out during their initial stage of recovery that they want to be 'traditional' women but feel inadequate and uncertain of their capacity in these roles, need insight-giving therapy to understand the source of their sense of inadequacy. They will then need to look at the setting within which they are happy to perform their traditional roles and see that it is dangerous to focus inwardly on the family in a total way, and to realize that however much they remain 'traditional' women, their security and health, in part, will lie in acknowledging and learning to admire and develop a self which can explore, change, and adapt, in relation to other experiences outside the family as well as within it. *This will be good for the family* as well as themselves and give them greater resources when the family need them less or if by change the family is suddenly disrupted. For them too, affiliating to extra-familial groups that have a meaning for them will help support their view of themselves as developing and interesting individuals, as well as wives and mothers.

Work with families

This section will cover work with families and work with parts of families such as the marital couple. The plight of the homeless woman will be discussed elsewhere but with them and single women, their loss of, or lack of, family will have a strong bearing on the counselling relationship and the external resources they will need.

The tendency for men to leave wives who are drinking excessively means that women drinkers are more likely to be single parents than are their male counterparts. This obviously raises a number of important issues. The problems encountered by the women drinker will become compounded with the problems facing all single parents and these multiple problems may in turn exacerbate the drinking. The question of the woman's ability to care adequately for her children causes a major headache for the helping agents involved in her treatment; social workers particularly find themselves asking the question of 'Who is the client?' and 'Where do their priorities lie?'. Is the major concern with the welfare of the children or the well-being of the mothers? Should the children be taken into care and what effect would such a move have on the relationship that can be maintained with the woman? Equally a woman drinker may be less than cooperative with a social worker when she knows the social worker has the power to take her children away. There is no pat-answer in this situation, which is all too familiar to the social work profession.

There are many reasons why attention must be paid to the families of all alcoholics, men and women, when attempting to understand, treat, and support during the recovery stage.

To begin with we have an obligation to respond to the suffering and distress of all those affected by drinking whether they be other family members or the drinkers themselves. Not only may the partners and children have suffered some years of disrupted and unhappy family life, but the children will be in danger of carrying this disturbance over into their adult life with the consequent perpetuation of unhappy relationships.

Moreover, when it comes to an objective examination of the effectiveness of what helps drinkers, and women drinkers in particular, this wider concern for families is further justified.

Although there are no conclusive findings, the work that has been done looking at families of drinkers (see chapter 5) indicates that the whole family should be involved in treatment if success is to be achieved. 'Success' should and needs to be not only related to drinking consumption but also to personal, family, and marital health. For women it is clear that this family related definition of success is inevitably intertwined with their own cure since this is where they generally see their problems and stresses and where they have often found their only sense of identity. They are also more inclined than men to be influenced by and dependent on their husband's view of their health and progress.

'Working with families' can mean many things and we need to be clear about aims and methods. Many social workers have developed a pattern of 'seeing families' which is vague and unclear both to the families and themselves. For instance, a counsellor may visit a woman drinker and merely hope to catch her husband or other family members in passing. This may provide some useful material regarding what happens in the home but it is not involving the family in treatment. Such casual, inexplicit behaviour can heighten anxiety and resistance within the family, allowing their fantasies to range from a sense of being spied on, to a resentment of the social relationship being given the drinker when they are having to live with her.

Similarly the 'long-term support' given to families can be worthless unless all share in and agree on the usefulness of that support and can see an end to it in view.

Family therapy based on general systems theory can be defined as the psychotherapeutic treatment of a natural social system, the family, using as its basic medium, conjoint interpersonal interviews (Walrond-Skinner, 1977). The significance of this treatment for alcoholics is that it involves a shift of focus from the individual and his or her illness to the family and their interactions. For those working with an 'illness-model' of alcoholism this is confusing and incompatible since the family as a whole is viewed as the client. It entails the counsellor using the whole of his or her psychodynamic make-up in a flexible, involved manner, entering into the family system as a human being with certain skills rather than as a professional. This may be a threat to those of us who value, and need, our detached professional cover.

But difficulties, if overcome, seem to point to a method of help that is not only valid for all alcoholics but would seem to be particularly helpful to women. Their acknowledged low self-esteem will surely be more likely to be lifted if problems are shared within the family rather than focused on them alone, and if we as their helpers are there with them as human beings.

The goals for treatment centre on an improvement in the functioning, flexibility, and growth potential of the family system as a whole rather than the more limited focus on reduction in drinking on the part of the identified patient.

As Walrond-Skinner points out, what distinguishes the systems theory approach from a psychoanalytic one is the concept of wholeness, and the dealing with the actual rather than the symbolic. Work is likely to concentrate more on the present, and the therapist's mandate is to help create that amount of family reorganization needed to support enduring family improvement. Work is likely to be highly structured and relatively short term, especially if task centred, and a contract of meetings is worked out from the beginning. Such a framework often proves reassuring to a family and encourages motivation and commitment for the family members who will value the clarity and authority of the therapist.

Marital therapy

The counselling of drinkers and their partners is practised more than family therapy, though the same vagueness and lack of clarity of method and aims can apply here. Partners of women drinkers are notoriously difficult to involve in treatment. They are said to show strong denial of the problem and may well be drinkers themselves. Every effort must be made to see them and their wives together in order for both the therapist and the couple to understand their relationship and the part alcohol plays in it and to consider the changes that need to be made. Again this is of particular importance for women with the strong link between their drinking and marital conflict.

Tamerin (1978: 199) observes:

'Rapid improvement in the clinical picture is more characteristic in conjoint marital treatment than in individual treatment of the female with a drinking problem. The reason for this is that the sharing of responsibility by the spouse and the willingness to make the effort to regularly attend the sessions does a great deal to rapidly diminish the patient's guilt and rage by opening channels for constructive communication, the development of mutual respect, and individual growth.'

In marital therapy as with family therapy it is realistic to be prepared, as counsellors, to face and feel some powerful and disturbing emotions. The sessions are a microcosmic expression of the family's, or couple's, continuous drama, and participation will mean knowing, being touched by, and sometimes being unable, for the moment, to do anything to lessen the pain in the family or between the couple.

In general it is best, for the same reasons as in group therapy, to work with another counsellor of the opposite sex. Contracts should be made together and kept to, though treatment may lead to mutually-agreed decisions to change the pattern of working by, say, seeing a sub-system of the family for a while, e.g. parents alone, or, in marital therapy, having some sessions where the couples split and see counsellors on their own.

Mention must be made here of Masters' and Johnson's marital therapy which concentrates on sexual dysfunction. This may well have a place in the treatment of women drinkers, because of the frequent sexual difficulties experienced by them and their partners.

Conclusions

The main methods of treatment have been described, within which various techniques may be used, and certain styles of approach and schools of thought followed. This can end up with women being offered little that helps them or can mean making use of this range to provide a well-planned and flexible approach to their individual needs. A woman drinker may benefit from a mixture of approaches, all having a purpose; she may be seen with her family for a series of family therapy sessions during which tasks will be set and the family members will all look at their behaviour and interaction; the woman drinker may be seen individually to work at her view of herself in her world and how she approaches life and situations in general. She may join a group and there practise new social skills and ways to assert herself as she experiments with social situations. She may then be helped to find resources other than a professional counsellor to provide real support for the steps ahead – AA, new friendships, women's groups.

Gomberg (1974: 183) states 'The assets of the patient and the concern of the therapist are I believe, the major determinants of effectiveness, not the treatment modality used'.

This statement focuses rightly on the importance of taking a positive view of our women clients and a critical one of ourselves and our attitudes as counsellors. But it is an indictment of either different counselling methods or our application of them if they are really inter-changeable or so shadowy in their intrinsic value. There would be a danger too in allowing that statement to lead us into complacency; instead we must continue to try to find the most appropriate ways of helping women drinkers to value themselves, to know what they want, to feel they have a right to ask for what they want, and then work with them to find ways of putting this into action.

References

Beckman, L.J. (1975) Women Alcoholics. *Journal of Studies on Alcoholism* **36**(7): 807 and 819.

Birchmore, D.F. and Walderman, R.L. (1975) The Woman Alcoholics: A Review. *The Ontario Psychologist* **7**(4): 10.

Curlee, J. (1968) Women Alcoholics. *Federal Probation* **32**: 16-20.

Gomberg, E.S. (1974) Women and Alcoholism. In V. Franks and V. Burtle (eds), *Women in Therapy: New Psychotherapies for a Changing Society*. New York: Plenum Press.

_____ (1976) Alcoholism in Women. In B. Kissin and H. Begleiter (eds), *The Biology of Alcoholism*. Vol. IV. *Social Aspects of Alcoholism*. New York: Plenum Press.

Halmos, P. (1978) *The Faith of the Counsellors*. London. Constable.

Lisansky, E.S. (1957) Alcoholism in Women: Social & Psychological Concomitants. Social History Data, *Quarterly Journal of Studies on Alcohol* **18**: 588-623.

Litman, G.K. and Wilson, C. (1978) *A Review of Services for Women Alcoholics in the U.K.* Paper presented at the 24th International Institute on the Prevention and Treatment of Alcoholism, Zurich.

Masters, W.H. and Johnson, V.E. (1965) Counselling with Sexually Incompatible Marriage Partners. In R.H. Klemer (ed.), *Counseling in Marital and Sexual Problems*. Baltimore, Maryland: Williams & Wilkins Company.

Mayer, J. and Green, M. (1967) Group Therapy of Alcoholic Women Ex-prisoners. *Quarterly Journal of Studies on Alcohol* **28**: 493-504.

Robinson, D. and Henry, S. (1977) Alcoholics Anonymous in England and Wales. *British Journal on Alcohol and Alcoholism* **13**: 36-44.

Sclare, A.B. (1975) The Women Alcoholics. *Journal of Alcoholism* **10**: 134.

Spratley, T.A. (1974) *Alcoholics – My Present Views*. Pamphlet issued by Camberwell Council on Alcoholism Library, London.

Steinglass, P. (1977) Family Therapy in Alcoholism. In B. Kissin and H. Begleiter (eds), *The Biology of Alcoholism*. Vol. 5. *Treatment and Rehabilitation of the Chronic Alcoholic*. New York: Plenum Press.

Tamerin, J.S. (1978) The Psychotherapy of Alcoholic Women. In S. Zinbergs, J. Wallace, S.B. Blume (eds), *Practical Approaches to Alcoholism Psychotherapy*. New York: Plenum Press.

Walrond-Skinner, S. (1977) *Family Therapy*. London: Routledge and Kegan Paul.

Wilsnack, S.C. (1973) Sex Role Identity in Female Alcoholism. *Journal of Abnormal Psychology* **82**(2): 260.

8

SHIRLEY OTTO

Research Psychologist
Detoxification Evaluation Unit
Maudsley Hospital, London

Single homeless women and alcohol

'The nature of the problem as it affects women is not essentially different from that we have described in relation to men and that the treatment facilities and arrangements we have proposed for the one are likely to prove as appropriate (or inappropriate) for the other.' (Home Office 1971: 160).

This chapter concerns women who broadly come within the three criteria: have an established alcohol problem, are not part of an intact family, and who regularly use cheap rented accommodation (whether provided commercially or by charities), government reception centres for the destitute, night shelters, or who sleep rough in derelict houses, etc. 'Single homeless people', 'habitual drunkenness offenders', 'public inebriates', and 'Skid Row alcoholics' are labels commonly used to describe the different women who come within the criteria. The labels tend to reflect the points of view about the women's life-style of the various authorities who encounter them.

As such labels are often used vaguely it is worth taking time to clarify as far as possible the definition adopted here:

(1) *The Single Homeless*. The 1966 National Assistance Board

survey, *Homeless Single Persons*, acknowledged the difficulties involved in defining this group and therefore

'decided that it would be best not to concentrate on descriptions of persons or social groups but to aim the survey broadly at the accommodation and situations where experience suggested that unsettled persons could be found. This approach meant covering the following field: persons sleeping rough, persons using Reception Centres, persons using lodging houses, hostels, and shelters, and persons seeking financial help from the Board's local offices when they were without accommodation.' (National Assistance Board 1966: 2)

This pragmatic approach was maintained in a 1972 survey carried out on behalf of the Department of Health and Social Security (DHSS), by Wingfield-Digby (1976). The definition is useful as it underlines that women should be considered homeless even when they have a permanent bed in a common lodging house or hostel. The emphasis on women who are not part of intact families is a reflection of prevailing legislation which gives a much lower priority to those in housing need if they are single as opposed to members of a family, especially one with children. The so-called protective legislation for homeless families requires that the single and homeless be regarded as separate, in terms of social policy. Consequently, reports and policy papers tend to consider one or other of these groups and not both. This book contains substantial material on alcoholism problems in families and as so little has been drawn together about single homelessness and alcoholism, this chapter will draw primarily from literature on single homelessness.

(2)   *Female Drunkenness Offenders.* A number of homeless women alcoholics are appropriately labelled habitual drunkenness offenders, as they do spend substantial amounts of time in court and in prison for drunkenness and for non-payment of fines for drunkenness. However, to be a homeless alcoholic does not necessarily mean the person is also habitually arrested for drunkenness offences nor that those who are offenders also have no 'home'.

This chapter will draw considerably from studies of the habitual drunkenness offender for two reasons. First, because much has already been written in previous chapters about female alcoholism and because, regrettably, there is very little literature on the homeless alcoholic woman apart from these penal studies.

Ironically, there is a small but substantial body of literature on the homeless alcoholic male based on studies in the USA and England. It is worth, briefly, examining this bias further; approximately nine research reports are available that focus on the homeless alcoholic woman. Two leading books on Skid Row Alcoholics by Wiseman (1970) and Archard (1976) mention women in the most cursory way, despite both claiming to be about Skid Row alcoholics *per se*. Wiseman mentions women in a chapter on survival strategies adopted by men to meet basic needs such as for food and shelter, and sex (hence the mention of women!). For her, women appear to have no significance outside the servicing of homeless men. Archard touches on homeless women twice, the longest mention is in the Appendix; he notes that women are not welcome by many of the men who drink in gangs as they do not appreciate the group 'rules' about sharing money and drink. The DHSS survey of single homeless accommodation, conducted by Wingfield-Digby (1976) and the Home Office Working Party (1971) report on drunkenness offenders, both discuss the problems of women in short chapters set apart from the main body of the text.

There is however a multitude of magazine articles, campaign documents, and information from surveys carried out by groups concerned to bring about changes in legislation for women, alcoholism, and the single homeless. More substantially there are research and policy papers on such topics as casual labour and primary health care for the single homeless from which conclusions can be inferred about the situation for women, thereby providing means to explore issues further, however tentatively.

At this point it is important to consider why this group of female alcoholics require a separate chapter when so much that has come before is clearly relevant to them. There are three reasons why this is necessary. First, studies of single homeless alcoholics stress the powerful environmental factors that shape the life-style of those involved to the extent that the most extreme form, Skid Row, has become regarded by sociologists as a distinct subculture. To quote Wiseman:

'Not only has Skid Row proved tenacious as a continuing urban pattern but the area and its culture are strikingly similar from city to city and from time period to time period. In fact, descriptions of Skid Row have been remarkably stable over the past 50 years: the filth and the stench of the hotels, the greasy cheapness of the restaurants, the litter in the streets, the concentration of 'low type' bars or 'dives'. All of these aspects are mentioned again and again in both the research and the romantic literature from the 1920s until today.' (Wiseman 1970: 4)

If being homeless significantly affects the nature of the drinking problems of males then it is reasonable to assert that it must affect women also albeit in different ways.

Second, experience has shown on many occasions that drunkenness in women, especially when it is attended by unpredictable and disturbed behaviour angers, upsets, and threatens both lay and professional people to a degree not found with the homeless *per se* or with alcoholic men. These attitudes must colour how homeless alcoholic women are regarded and the extent to which they are 'seen' and therefore provision made for them.

Third, it has been common for the view (reflected in the introductory quote) to be taken that it is legitimate to assume that the problems of homeless alcoholic women are the same as those of men and that therefore planning for one invariably means planning for the other. Clearly, it is bad policy-making to make such assumptions when so little information is available, especially as what research is available has shown female alcoholism to be qualitatively different from alcoholism in men.

It is important then to draw together what is known so that a more competent assessment of the needs of these women can be made and services appropriately provided. What follows is an attempt to examine the issues associated with alcoholism amongst single homeless women by drawing on the various pockets of information on single homeless women and drunkenness offenders, so as to consider what can be gleaned, in the context of what is known about women with alcoholism problems. To do this is not ideal but to date it has to be enough.

1. Single homelessness

Single people have special problems in obtaining housing. The private rented sector, which has traditionally provided most single person accommodation, has declined dramatically. At the same time single people form a large and fast growing section of housing demand. Local authority building programmes have not been geared to the needs of single people and those unable to obtain a mortgage or local authority tenancy have over recent years found increased difficulty in finding accommodation. In 1947, 61 per cent of households in England and Wales lived in privately-rented accommodation. In 1961 the number had reduced to 27 per cent and by 1971 to approximately 14 per cent. The proportion of single person households has risen from 10 per cent in 1951 to 22.5 per cent in 1973. Local authorities have a statutory duty to provide housing for families with children and have tended to rely heavily on their housing waiting lists for information about housing needs (despite the fact that up until recently the points system used, discriminated against mobile single people without children). Such a system reflects only the needs of those who make demands, which in turn is greatly influenced by what people think is probably available to them. Single people have often considered it hardly worth applying for housing and have therefore remained undetected as a group in need.

This huge decline in private rented accommodation (made more acute by government legislation protecting the rights of tenants), and the loss of much large-scale cheap accommodation due to redevelopment, has created serious competition amongst single people for what little is left available. One of the effects has been to force many of those living in the twilight world of homelessness (i.e. in common lodging houses and hostels) who are poor and disabled, to have to live in 'skippers' (derelict houses) and/or government institutions for the destitute.

The means to alleviate the situation have been slow in coming because of such factors as local authority priorities for housing families and because the housing needs of single people have not been monitored in any way as to make their needs clear and of any paramount importance. It is only of late with the creation of a third sector of housing in the form of Housing Associations (which if appropriately registered receive central government subsidies for the provision of secure housing at a reasonable cost), have any changes been brought about to influence the availability of accommodation to single people whether they are homeless or not.

Homeless women have inevitably been affected by this process and perhaps more so, as much less cheaper accommodation had existed for them in the form of common lodging houses and hostels. One of the reasons that there has been so much more cheap accommodation for men is that this type of accommodation flourished in the last century in response to the need of poor working men and itinerant labour such as the Railway Navvies.

The Wingfield-Digby survey (1976) updated the census of homeless single person accommodation by the National Assistance Board (1966). The 1972 survey in addition reported on the material conditions and the characteristics of those people using common lodging houses/hostels. Forty-eight per cent of the establishments visited in 1966 were found to have closed down, which in effect meant a loss of 36 per cent of all beds. However, this loss was counterbalanced by the opening of new hostels particularly in the non-statutory sector where there was a gain of 16 per cent of the total number of beds. By far the biggest overall loss occurred in the commercial sector. Unfortunately, the survey did not separate out the loss of beds for women as compared to those for men. However, it is clear that in 1972 the number of beds for women were far fewer than those for men (25,561 were men, 2,273 for women and 3,301 were available for either sex). The non-statutory sector (e.g. Salvation and Church armies) supplied almost three quarters of the total beds for women while commercial interests only provided 14 per cent.

Conditions in lodging houses for either sex were found to be very poor indeed. For example, a very high proportion lacked adequate washing or toilet facilities.

One in ten of residents in all common lodging houses and hostels visited were approached for interview (83 per cent were successfully interviewed); of this sample 172 were women, that is 8·6 per cent of the total sample. Of these 54 per cent were single, 28 per cent had been divorced or separated, and 17 per cent were widowed. In many ways the women appeared to be a fairly settled group as 43 per cent had been in the same hostel or boarding house for over two years. Many more women than men were found to have been referred by an agency to their particular common lodging house or hostel. Almost as many women as men gave their last settled address as their parental home with the rest mentioning their marital homes, relatives, or friends. They were also more likely to have been in contact with relatives, with approximately 15 per cent having been in touch in the previous four weeks. The importance of close ties was further stressed as women particularly said they valued good relationships with other residents and staff. They stood out in stressing their dislike of any lack of privacy. Many said that given the chance they would prefer to live in flats where they would have a greater opportunity for privacy, independence, and a sense of ownership.

At the time of the survey (1972) 55 per cent of the women under sixty said that they had a job, compared with 43 per cent of the men. Their social class, as determined by their present job, showed the women to differ markedly from the men. A third of the women were in skilled non-manual jobs compared with 5 per cent of the men; 20 per cent of the women had kept their present job for at least a year, as had a similar proportion of the men. Eighteen per cent of the women who were unable to work said it was due to illness and 17 per cent said that they could not find employment or had young children to look after.

Very few had been in hospital in the last two years and almost none in the last two months. Of those that had been in hospital a quarter said it was due to some form of mental illness or depression. A complementary survey of the Supplementary Benefits Commission Records showed that 10 per cent of the women had a record of a spell in hospital as an in-patient (although usually some years ago), and 44 per cent were recorded as having received sickness benefit because of a 'mental illness, neurosis, nervous disability, or similar diagnosis which may indicate mental illness' (Wingfield-Digby 1976: 214).

Wingfield-Digby concluded that over half of the women living in common lodging houses or hostels had some record of emotional or psychiatric problem, although only a small percentage had actually been in mental hospital. Fewer women than men (10 per cent compared to to 36 per cent) had ever been in prison, approved school, or remand home. Unfortunately, Wingfield-Digby did not tease out imprisonment for drunkenness offences nor as is indicated above, treatment for alcohol problems.

It would appear that the women using these common lodging houses and hostels had a more stable life-style, in terms of retaining accommodation and work, than might have been expected. The extent to which the women suffered from alcohol problems cannot be gauged. It is reasonable to assume however that few of these women were disruptive enough to be evicted and/or banned or had suffered acute illnesses due to heavy drinking. It might then be summarized that, in fact, few women with serious drinking problems were found in these hostels and common lodging houses, but that they would have been found had the survey extended to those sleeping rough or using Government Reception Centres. This speculation is consistent with research into characteristics of users of various kinds of cheap accommodation for men. Tidmarsh and Wood (1972) in their study of the new and repeated admissions of homeless men at the Camberwell Reception Centre concluded that few alcoholics were tolerated by common lodging house managers, because of their drunken and aggressive behaviour, and they therefore had to sleep rough, in derelict houses, etc.

Further evidence that this might be the case is presented in an article by Brandon (1973) which describes one of the few non-statutory projects for homeless women, based in central London. This project is described as having been set up to cater for the most destitute of women. Brandon conducted a brief, albeit somewhat unsystematic, survey of all those residents there on two separate days, four months apart. On the first of the days the forty-six residents were found to be either young or old (i.e. up to twenty years old, or over fifty years old). Many had had psychiatric treatment, while just under a third had convictions of some sort. Most had never been married and few had had children. On the second of the days there were forty-eight residents, (it would appear that just under half were the same people) who showed the same age distribution, history of psychiatric treatment, and convictions. There were rather more disabled women than on the previous day. Brandon commented that many of the women had come to the project via a common route.

For various reasons they had come to require hospitalization, but after leaving hospital they had few personal contacts and fairly quickly started an unsettled life in cheap accommodation. He regarded psychiatric treatment as having 'apparently done nothing to arrest their downward slide' (Brandon 1973: 176).

The women who used this project were in many ways more unstable than those using the common lodging houses, etc. described by Wingfield-Digby. It is not without coincidence that this form of accommodation is regarded as equivalent to living on the streets if not worse by some.

In 1975 the Leeds Cyrenians Association (Matthews 1975) carried out a survey of homeless women in Leeds with a view to establishing a house for the groups found in most need. The survey is particularly interesting as it collected information from those agencies who referred homeless women and it followed up the outcome. It was an attempt to assess need from the point of view of demand rather than from the take-up of what is provided.

The survey was conducted over a period of a month and involved twenty-nine referral agents who in that time attempted to find accommodation for eighty-one cases (made up of forty-seven single women, thirty-one families, and three childless couples). This total was regarded by the authors as an under-estimate because not all the agencies seeking accommodation for women in Leeds were included as some were based in other cities; self referrals were not monitored nor those by ordinary citizens, and finally, the authors had doubts about the quality of the forms that were filled in, given that some agencies seemed none too clear about the purpose of the research.

Of all the women interviewed, thirty-eight were clearly single homeless and the outcome of the referrals of these women was as follows:

fifteen were placed
seventeen were not placed
three were of unknown outcome
three – no information

The largest proportion of those unplaced were old and infirm. Two thirds of those placed were sent to hostels or common lodging houses.

Unfortunately, few details were provided as to how many of

the women had drinking problems. However, the authors comment:

> 'The provision may have shaped the demand. Thus, apparently, only two alcoholic women were encountered during the sample month and there was "no demand" for an alcoholism hostel despite Cyrenian experience of the number of women with drinking problems. Hence the conclusion could only be drawn that because no provision existed for women with alcohol problems the referring agents did not see fit to use that particular label, however appropriate.' (Matthews, 1975: 43)

Placing the individual homeless women was found to be more difficult on the whole than placing couples or families. This was particularly the case for those women with special problems such as 'mental illness, depression or subnormality'. Women with a history of drifting or rootlessness were about the most difficult to place, especially as it was found that conventional hostels were reluctant to take women of this kind. These problems were further compounded by the fact that many were also elderly as well.

SOME CONCLUSIONS

(1) Sufficient homelessness exists amongst women to warrant attention. This is particularly important given the issue of provision shaping demand as was indicated by the Leeds Cyrenian survey. Many of the women referred for accommodation in Leeds could not be appropriately described as either single or as a family for they had just left a partner and/or children. Such women were often in need of temporary accommodation perhaps of the kind provided by Womens Aid for those in need of refuge because they had been battered by their husbands.

(2) Homeless women living in street level accommodation such as that described by Brandon have and do suffer considerable physical and psychiatric problems more so than their counterparts in common lodging houses and hostels. They would appear to be particularly disadvantaged if they have long histories of psychiatric hospital admissions, if they are elderly, or have had a rootless style of life.

This suggests there may be a hierarchy of accommodation available according to a woman's capacity to earn her living and to remain acceptable to those who run the various institutions. Once a woman has become old, ill, or overtly distressed she is less able to retain such accommodation and ultimately has no other choice but to exist at street level. It is safe to conclude that those living in this way are only the 'tip of the iceberg' and that they must have been affected by the downward process through various institutions largely hidden from view.

(3)   Although little mention is made in the various surveys of alcoholism the high rates of psychiatric admissions and convictions suggest that alcohol problems are present amongst those no longer using common lodging houses, etc. because they have been banned. It is likely that the surveys omitted to ask questions about drinking problems because for so long it has been assumed that alcoholism is predominantly the prerogative of the male. This assumption is not peculiar to those working with or indeed studying the homeless woman as can be seen from other chapters.

2.   Habitual drunkenness offenders

Homelessness does not necessarily equate with criminality. However, many who are homeless do become involved in the penal system to an extent unparalleled by those who have a home. Homeless persons are often on the streets and therefore liable to be apprehended when drinking or drunk. Fortunately, there are studies of women caught up in the penal system although the studies tend to focus on small groups who habitually offend.

Woodside (1961) studied twenty-six women admitted to Holloway Prison on charges connected with drunkenness. She obtained information from records and interviews. She found the women to be mostly middle-aged, of social classes four and five (the commonest occupation was catering and unskilled domestic work), and when not in prison primarily users of cheap accommodation. Many had been married but all were by that time separated or divorced. All had previous convictions with three having more than a hundred and nine more than forty convictions. Although the majority of the convictions were for drunkenness, twelve had been convicted of prostitution, fourteen of larceny, and others for wilful damage, assaulting police, and in one case of causing grievous bodily harm. Woodside pointed out that this latter kind of criminal behaviour was very much in the women's past, as with the development of chronic alcoholism they had come only to be arrested for drunkenness.

Their mental and physical health was very poor. VD, infections and physical deformities and handicaps were common and only three women were regarded as having 'nothing abnormal about their mental state'. She described them as drinking cheap wine and regarded by officials as aggressive/abusive/irritable, and anti-social.

d'Orban (1969) studied women described by officers at Holloway Prison as habitual drunkenness offenders, over a four-year period. These women had spent more time in prison than at liberty. In fact, these women dominated the reception statistics as they accounted for 10 per cent of the annual receptions to the prison during the four year period of study. The women were mainly sentenced for accumulated fines imposed for drunkenness, street offences, (e.g. begging and tresspass), wilful damage, and assault on the police. Only four had had convictions for soliciting and none recently.

In nearly all respects this group of women mirrored those described by Woodside. Their health was very poor, their income came irregularly from casual work and Supplementary Benefits (SB) payments. d'Orban found they also supplemented their income through casual associations with men which may have something to do with the finding that they claimed less SB payments than they were entitled to. This was partly due to the difficulty encountered when claiming without a fixed abode. This situation was further worsened, in his view, by their reluctance to use certain hostels and reception centres and by the fact they were so often banned anyway.

Prince (1969: 61) looked in some detail at the relationship between offences of prostitution and drunkenness. Her work led her to conclude: 'a number of differences will probably be found between the serious alcoholic who prostitutes in order to get money for drink on the one hand, and the professional prostitute who is also a heavy drinker on the other.'

The experience of the Leeds Cyrenian workers is that:

'homeless women often turn to sugar daddies to depend on. This would be a man who is tapped and picked up in a pub, thereby getting at least temporary shelter, bed and money. It can be a social worker or probation officer, to sort out and take responsibility for a woman's practical and emotional problems, it can be a Cyrenian, it can be the local G.P., the drugs he prescribes and it can often be the mental hospital.' (Leeds Cyrenian Association 1977: 3)

There is little information available about women who are not habitual drunkenness offenders but who are imprisoned and who have an alcohol problem. However, the study by Prince suggests what might come to light should such studies be conducted. Prince interviewed one in four of all women received into Holloway prison in one year. During the interview the women were asked whether they had a drink problem and if so to what extent. Of the total sample of 637 women, 161 (25·6 per cent) had a drink problem. Prince regarded this 25·6 per cent as falling into three main categories:
1.   Forty-nine (8 per cent) who came to prison as a result of a drunkenness charge.
2.   Twenty-seven (4·2 per cent) who came into the sample on a non drink charge but were known to have at least one previous conviction for drunkenness.
3.   Eighty-five (13·4 per cent) who came to prison on a non drink charge, were not known to have previous convictions for drunkenness, but who described themselves as 'quite heavy drinkers' or as 'drinking too much'.
Prince held there to be a relationship between a woman's age and the number of times she has been convicted for drunkenness. Those admitted on a drunkenness charge tended to be older than those who had no recorded convictions for drunkenness but who were none the less heavy drinkers. This led the Habitual Drunkenness Offenders Working Party (Home Office 1971: 165) to conclude:

'It is a fair assumption that a proportion of the latter group will in the years to come be making a contribution to the drunkenness statistics. The findings are further evidence of the need for diagnosis and treatment to be carried out before the stage at which a serious drinking problem manifests itself in drunkenness offences as such.'

A study by Schuckit and Morrissey (1979) of women admitted to a detoxification centre in the USA suggests further evidence that women convicted for drunkenness are only the tip of the 'alcoholic' iceberg. Schuckit and Morrissey found that 13 per cent of women admitted could not be clearly diagnosed as alcoholics although they showed patterns of heavy drinking and were found to have alcohol-related health problems.

Prince studied the appearance of women at two selected London courts over a three-month period. (These courts were found to contribute a third of the annual intake into Holloway prison.) Fifty per cent of all female offenders dealt with at one court were all apprehended for drunkenness again. The offenders were a small group of women usually middle aged and homeless. Of the ninety-three women who appeared in the courts during the three months only one was recommended for medical or social enquiry. d'Orban concluded that there was 'evidence to suggest that female offenders, although small in number, are a relatively more serious problem in courts and prisons than their male counterparts' (d'Orban 1969: 51). Walker (1965) found that women habitual drunkenness offenders made up 13 per cent to 18 per cent of annual receptions into Holloway prison which was twice the rate for drunkenness offences found amongst male prisoners. Again, the recurrent picture is of a small group of women consuming a considerable amount of court and prison time.

With this conclusion in mind it is important to consider the outcome of arrests of home-based women who appear before the courts for drunkenness. A survey of the records of three London courts for the months of January to July 1979 was carried out by Peterson and Richmond (1979). They found that the women apprehended were predominantly home-based, if somewhat tenuously in high-grade lodging house accommodation. Schuckit and Morrissey (1979) reported that only 9·9 per cent of the women diagnosed as primary alcoholics (53 per cent of the total sample) lived on 'Skid Row'. Steele (1978) extracted information from the records of four London-based agencies for alcoholics, all of which primarily served home-based men and women. (The four agencies were: a hospital in-patient unit, two day centres, and a counselling service.) Whereas few women who had been admitted to the hospital had one or more offences for drunkenness, (7·5 per cent), rather more women who had been so convicted attended the day centres and most so convicted used the counselling service (84·6 per cent of twenty-four cases).

It might tentatively be concluded that whereas home-based women do on occasions get apprehended by the police for drunkenness they are not necessarily convicted nor committed to prison to the same extent as homeless women. Steele (1978: appendix) quotes a London based Chief Superintendent of the police as stating 'We do not charge women unless we really have to, we get them home and tell them to go and see their doctor'. This attitude of the police towards home-based women alcoholics was noted by Schuckit and Morrissey (1979) and Perry (1979) with female addicts and is consistent with criminological research. If women are apprehended, (for whatever crime), they are more likely to be found not guilty or given non-custodial sentences. For example, of 3,868 women and girls remanded in 1977, 2,693 were found not guilty or given non-custodial sentences. This is the case for far fewer men (Howard League for Penal Reform, 1979).

The reluctance of police to apprehend and the courts to convict women would appear only to extend to home-based women. The studies of Prince, Woodside, and d'Orban all suggest that if a woman is homeless (with all that this entails in terms of her appearance and behaviour), she is very likely to be arrested and convicted.

SOME CONCLUSIONS

(1)   The three major studies quoted are at one in identifying a small hard core group of women who are drunkenness offenders. d'Orban describes these women as dependent on prison as an institution. They clearly have severe alcohol problems, very poor health, and are in all respects a most incapacitated group, so much so that it is a wonder that no alternative provision has been created for them.

(2)   It is reasonable to speculate that a form of discrimination is practised by the police and courts that favours home-based women who are apprehended for drunkenness. Home-based women are worthy of a 'protection' not 'merited' by homeless women.

(3)   It is clear that being homeless is of itself a debilitating process both physically and emotionally. In many cases economic survival requires a degree of casual prostitution, a phenomenon unknown in male homeless alcoholics. The use of this means of survival cannot be separated from the conditions in which these women live and it is important in considering why the women are so long in becoming visible on the streets. Many are able to remain hidden from view through such casual associations as long as their health and looks prevail; then, as Woodside and d'Orban show, their range of convictions, including soliciting, narrows with increasing age and infirmity until they are only convicted for drunkenness.

3.a)   Provision

Chapter 6, 'Response and recognition', has outlined the range of services available, or not, for women alcoholics. The role of this section is to reflect on what is described there in terms of the single homeless woman, and to consider the attitudes of those providing the services about such women.

(i) SPECIALIST STATUTORY SERVICES

Alcoholism Treatment Units (ATU): Homeless people, whatever their sex, are only infrequently admitted to ATUs. The homeless alcoholic tends to be regarded as insufficiently articulate to cope with the demands of group therapy, (the prevailing type of treatment in ATUs). As the men particularly are often of social classes four/five, it is assumed they will not mix well with more middle-class, home-based, alcoholics. Perhaps the most cogent argument is the problem faced by hospital social workers in finding them appropriate accommodation once they have completed the treatment programme. It is not uncommon for homeless alcoholics not to be accepted into an ATU unless such accommodation is guaranteed by the agent of referral. This form of discrimination would affect women as much as men, although the degree will vary depending on which sex is most provided for locally.

Detoxification Services: Detoxification services have only recently been made available, in any comprehensive form, to the homeless alcoholic. One of the two Detox Centres set up as part of a central Government experiment admits women. This unit, along with other hospital-based detox services, is in fact the only specialist service to admit women. The non-statutory projects, such as those run by the Salvation Army, do not.

(ii) SPECIALIST NON-STATUTORY COUNSELLING SERVICES

Few homeless alcoholic women use counselling services whether provided either as part of a day centre or a Council on Alcoholism. These agencies primarily cater for the home-based problem drinker. It is often the intention of such services to so discriminate as it is again considered unhelpful to mix homeless and homebased people. The form of provision considered most appropriate to providing day services for the homeless are called 'shop fronts' (pioneered by the Alcoholic Recovery Project) and recommended by the 1971 *Habitual Drunken Offenders Report* (Home Office, 1971). They are intended to be easily accessible to the homeless (i.e. they are situated where the homeless congregate) and generic in approach, thereby giving the homeless access to the medical, social work, and psychiatric care they require. However, as sensible as this type of service would appear, very few have been established. Those that do exist are only infrequently used by homeless alcoholic women for reasons that are not, as yet, clearly understood but may have something to do with reports from shop front staff that men do not tend to make the women welcome.

(iii) RESIDENTIAL FACILITIES

Chapter 6 mentions the limited number of beds available for women alcoholics in residential facilities, especially in single-sex establishments. It is therefore not surprising that there is even less for those women who are also homeless. If anything, the women are likely to be given a roof over their head and some support by the few agencies catering for all types of women who are homeless.

(iv) ALCOHOLICS ANONYMOUS (AA)

Woodside found that many of the women she interviewed had attended AA but were reluctant to use it on any regular basis.

(v) NON-SPECIALIST STATUTORY SERVICES

Health Services: Hewetson (1976) and Campaign for the Homeless and Rootless (1977) amongst others, have demonstrated how little use the homeless can make of the General Practitioner system, with the effect that they tend to use casualty departments, if anything at all. This is to be expected as the GP system like local authority housing, is geared to people living a settled way of life. GPs too, tend to be reluctant to have homeless people in any numbers in their waiting rooms, as their dishevelled appearance and sometimes strange behaviour can offend. Some are also aware that, even should they see the homeless, a far greater range of skills and knowledge may be required than they have to offer.

Over the last few years, it has become the trend for agencies catering for the homeless to have a doctor available for a number of sessions per week. This response is not only to do with the need of this group for primary medical care, but also because already over-burdened casualty departments tend to treat them in a rather perfunctory fashion.

Little is known about what help, if any, homeless women receive for gynaecological problems, when they are pregnant or want an abortion.

The difficulties experienced by homeless alcoholic women in obtaining primary health care must contribute to the very poor health found amongst the women studied, in Holloway Prison, by d'Orban and Woodside.

Social Services Departments: Local authority social services departments, like housing departments, allocate priority to families (especially those with children), and to the elderly and the disabled. Few homeless people appear to make use of local social services area offices, except occasionally to obtain financial help or clothing. Lack of provision for the single homeless can cause social workers to respond in a similar way as they do to alcoholics. The work of Shaw, Cartwright, Spratley and Jarwin (1979) showed how local authority social workers, amongst others, preferred not to detect, and therefore take on, problems for which no means of help was available.

Probation Service: The probation service is probably the most in touch with homeless alcoholic women because so many are, at times, offenders. In a sense, the probation service is the statutory social work service for the homeless particularly in areas where there is a Homeless Offenders Unit. These units not only assist homeless people on probation, but any homeless who have at any time been on their books.

b)   Attitudes to working with homeless alcoholic women

'Never wear a tie when homeless women are around because as likely as not they will strangle you with it.' (Staff member, Church of Scotland Night Shelter, for men)

Two myths prevail about homeless alcoholic women: that they are more violent and unpredictable than men and that they have a very poor prognosis.

Single homeless women are often described as violent, unpredictable, and difficult to control, particularly those who are alcoholic. d'Orban and Woodside both regarded the women they studied as having 'strongly anti-authoritarian attitudes' (d'Orban 1969: 61). (Hence they considered the reason so many of the women were banned from lodging houses, etc.) It is interesting that this opinion is not contradicted by staff working in less authoritatian settings, although they are more likely to give the reasons for this behaviour as social rather than pathological. For example, a pamphlet about 'Settles Street' (one of the few residential facilities for homeless alcoholic women) purports to speak for the women:

'They might also lash out, resist their oppressive environment, hit out blindly at people, authority, smash windows, property, people. Have you ever heard someone say "I just could not bear to be told what to do again – I just epxloded".

Given this perpetually oppressive environment, these women have continually found themselves hitting out at parent figures. Never getting the opportunity to think for themselves, they become more alienated, their behaviour more unacceptable, society more oppressive, and on and on and on.' (Lloyd 1976: 8)

The staff at the Leeds Cyrenian House for women share this perspective, although they express it rather less passionately:

'Nevertheless, the powerlessness is there, D.H.S.S., Housing, the Courts, Social Services, are often frightening, even though they all provide a helping service. I am sure this is bound up with the authority invested in these bodies. They are all so frightening because of their show of power – particularly the first three bodies mentioned, with their huge office blocks, formal procedures, bureaucratic structures and mysterious ways of moving.' (Leeds Cyrenian Association, 1977: 3)

There is as yet too little evidence to say whether, as a group, homeless alcoholic women are indeed more violent and unpredictable than their male counterparts, (if it is ever possible to prove it), for it takes more than one person to create a drama, especially when there is violence. It is not uncommon for police and male workers to say that they feel themselves inhibited when dealing with homeless alcoholic women as they cannot 'manhandle' women with the same ease as men. Some are reported as saying that they fear the women will take advantage of them, when they are alone, by accusing them of rape. The women, too, are often in a minority in the mixed-sex agencies, therefore their behaviour is more noticeable, more often remembered and commented on.

The combination of alcohol problems and homelessness in women has invariably led to the assumption that little improvement is possible and therefore only basic support and shelter need be offered. This is despite research (Otto and Orford, 1978) on social work agencies for homeless alcoholic men, (who had long been considered untreatable), which show small but real achievements. The assumption that the homeless alcoholic woman is even more hopeless than the male may be to do with the common image of her as either a deranged old woman pushing a cartful of old newspapers or as a slut living in a seedy bed-sitter dressed in a soiled slip, with a cigarette dangling from her lips, and occasionally swigging from a bottle of spirits. There *are* unpleasant stereotypes at large about the male homeless person that reflect considerable hostility and vehemence against, to use a favourite phrase in accusatory letters to newspapers, the 'dregs and derelicts of society'. Yet, at the same time, there are quite romantic images of the male, no less biased, most often found in sociological literature, attributing to them the qualities of noble savages. There is a small, but coherent, body of literature that celebrates the lives of male hobos, tramps, and drifters, (for example Anderson, 1923; Kerouac 1962; and Orwell 1933). Unfortunately, no such sentiment would appear to have rubbed off on the women. They excite no-one's fantasy or envy (Harwin and Otto, 1979).

The women may excite anger in some, but more typically pity which is often expressed by those in authority in a form of paternalism. Articles in popular magazines often provide the best example of this attitude. For example, in a short story entitled 'Coup de Grace' by Diana Quay (1979), a homeless woman is approached in Portobello Market by the police . . . 'She could hardly see the uniform for the tears. She could hardly hear what he was saying, for the sobs. But she knew he must be asking her her name. They always did. She waited for him to make a joke about her surname. They always did. One of them had her suitcase. The other was leaning down, trying to cheer her up.

"It's alright, Maggie!" It was Marge, not Maggie. But it was all the same in the end. "Come on then love. Everything's fine."

He was young, the Bobby. He didn't know. He didn't know nothing could ever be fine again. Her anger at this approach to her, at the people who 'never spoke to you directly, never answered you, at the most they just looked' is deep and long-felt. She is moved on by the police:

'She could feel the firmness of the hands at her elbow. They were moving past the stalls and she'd stopped sobbing. Now she was crooning her own nameless song again. Letting it grow big and round. Big enough to hurl it at the enquiring faces passing by.'

Finally, inherent in the assumption that these women are, as a group, volatile and unpredictable, is to see them as child-like and therefore unable to be responsible for themselves, as would be expected of an adult. Consequently, it is assumed that what the women want is not important, at least not as important as the views of those who deal with them. In the words of Adrian Jones (1977: 5), writing about his work at the Leeds Cyrenian House: 'it's all there in that statement – the utter reasonableness of saying "it is not what you want, but what we say you need".' In his view, this effectively puts women off, for he comments that it is: 'not surprising then that even at our house – a liberal institution . . . 39 people wandered: not surprising that 45 out of 100 we knew wandered from hostel to hostel, and town to town on the round-about of homelessness.'

From this perspective, it could be argued that the women's 'difficult' behaviour would be better understood as an assertion of independence, arising out of a desire for self-determination none too clearly communicated. To quote Adrian Jones (1977: 5) again:

'They have overwhelmingly shunned hostels and Cyrenian Houses as in any way being an acceptable, permanent life-style. They have elected, rather, for privacy and independence. Some 60 out of 100 people who lived at our house in its first year wanted to live in flats, bed-sits, and private houses. But the referring agencies are not geared to helping homeless women in this way; so the women are denied opportunity and money and practical help to live how they want.'

Discussion

The authors of the Habitual Drunkenness Offenders Report (Home Office 1971: 160) assumed that 'The nature of the problem as it affects women is not essentially different from that we have described in relation to men'. This assumption has not been borne out by the evidence presented in this chapter, which suggests that their advice has ill informed policy makers. Clearly, it is dangerous to assume similarities, or indeed differences, between groups of people with alcohol problems without thorough investigations.

More broadly, it could be argued that the most difficult problems confronted by homeless alcoholic women have arisen out of the assumptions made, by lay and professional people, about the nature of their problems. By virtue of being homeless women and being drunk in public they challenge expectations of appropriate female behaviour to such an extent that there has been a distinct prejudice against them. They are twice deviant; they are stigmatized for being drunk in public and for being seen to exist outside a family network. Curiously, they are considered to be 'mad or sad but never bad' (to modify a phrase used by Archard in his book (1976) on the homeless alcoholic male). They are perceived as children who do not know what is best for them; it is not allowed that their behaviour might have some validity in terms of how they have tried to meet the problem of survival. At best the women are to be 'protected' and patronized, at worst regarded as non-people, devoid of anything positively associated with the labels 'person', 'woman', or 'adult'.

It can only be concluded that the apparent indifference to the problems of homeless alcoholic women has as much as anything to do with the acute discomfort created by members of the 'gentle sex' being overtly drunk, bawling, and fighting for all their lives are worth. The improvement of health, housing, and social services for these women will not only require further research work as to their needs but more significantly a change in political attitudes about women's situation and how this is related to their individual problems. This change in attitude is even more important because the needs of this group have only come to light of late and at a time when even basic health services are being cut back. However, cuts or no cuts, it is indisputable that homeless alcoholic women have rights to health, housing, and social service provision and should be seen to be worthy of them, simply because, as people, they need them.

References

Anderson, N. (1923) *The Hobo: The Sociology of the Homeless Man*. Chicago: University of Chicago Press.

Archard, P. (1976) *The Bottle Won't Leave You*. London: Alcoholics Recovery Project.

Brandon, D. (1973) Community for Homeless Women. *Social Work Today* 4(6): 167-170.

Campaign for the Homeless and Rootless (1977). *Health Care Need of Homeless People*. CHAR Submission to the Royal Commission on the National Health Service. CHAR.

Harwin, J. and Otto, S.J. (1979) Women, Alcohol and the Screen. In J. Cook and M. Lewington (eds), *Images of Alcoholism*. London: British Film Institute/Alcohol Education Centre.

Hewetson, J. (1976). Long Term Reception Centre users as an At Risk Group. A Report by the Visiting Medical Officer. Unpublished Paper Submitted to DHSS.

Home Office (1971) *Habitual Drunkenness Offenders: Working Party Report*. London: HMSO.

Howard League for Penal Reform (1979) Memo to the House of Commons Expenditure Committee. Minutes of the House of Commons Expenditure Committee. March 1979. London: HMSO.

Jones, A. (1977) These Women Want Houses. Yes, But What do They Need? *National Cyrenians Newsletter*. February 1977: 5.

Kerouac, J. (1962) *Lonesome Traveller*. St Albans: Panther Books Limited.

Leeds Cyrenian Association, (1977) *One Year of Oakdale House – Homeless Single Women and Couples in Leeds*. Leeds: Leeds Cyrenian Association.

Lloyd, T. (1976) Settles Street: 5 Years On. *Homeless in Britain*. Published by Christian Publications Limited.

Matthews, G. (1975). *Homeless Women In Leeds – Past, Present and Future*. Leeds: Leeds Cyrenians Association.

National Assistance Board (1966) *Homeless Single Persons* London: HMSO.

d'Orban, P.T. (1969) Habitual Drunkenness Offenders in Holloway Prison. In T. Cook, D. Gath, and C. Hensman (eds), *The Drunkenness Offence*. London: Pergamon Press.

Orwell, G. (1933) *Down and Out in Paris and London*. London: Gollancz.

Otto, S.J. and Orford, J. (1978) *Not Quite Like Home: A Study of Small Hostels for Alcoholics and Others*. Chichester: J. Wiley and Sons Ltd.

Perry, L. (1979) *Women and Drug Use – an Unfeminine Dependency*. Internal Paper prepared for the Institute for the Study of Drug Dependence, London.

Peterson, A. and Richmond, F. (1979) Female Drunkenness Offenders: A Survey of Three London Courts Records. *Occasional Paper No. 3*. London: Camberwell Council on Alcoholism.

Prince, J. (1969) Drinking Habits of Women in Holloway Prison and Those Dealt with at a London Court. In T. Cook, D. Gath, and C. Hensman (eds), *The Drunkenness Offence*. London: Pergamon Press.

Quay, D. (1979) Coup de Grace. A Short Story. *The Guardian*. July 9, 1979.

Schuckit, M.A. and Morrissey, E.R. (1979) Psychiatric Problems in Women Admitted to an Alcoholic Detoxification Centre. *American Journal of Psychiatry* **136**: (4D), 611-617.

Shaw, S., Cartwright, A.K.J., Spratley, T., and Harwin, J. (1978) *Responding to Drinking Problems*. London: Croom Helm.

Steele, D. (1978) Feminism and Social Policy. Thesis submitted for MA in Deviance and Social Policy, Middlesex Polytechnic.

Tidmarsh, D. and Wood, S. (1972) *Report on Research at Camberwell Reception Centre*. Medical Research Council Social Psychiatry Unit, Institute of Psychiatry. Unpublished Report submitted to the DHSS, London.

Walker, N. (1965) *Crime and Punishment in Britain*. Edinburgh: Edinburgh University Press.

Wingfield-Digby, P. (1976) *Hostels and Lodgings for Single People*. Offices of Population Censuses and Surveys. Social Survey Division. London: HMSO.

Wiseman, J.P. (1970) *Stations of the Lost: The Treatment of Skid Row Alcoholics*. New Jersey: Prentice-Hall, Inc.

Woodside, N. (1961) Women Drinkers Admitted to Holloway Prison During February 1960; A Pilot Survey. *British Journal of Criminology* **1**: 221-235.

Name index

Subject index